LUCRETIUS

LUCRETIUS
POET & PHILOSOPHER

by

E. E. SIKES

*Fellow and President of
St John's College
Cambridge*

CAMBRIDGE
AT THE UNIVERSITY PRESS
1936

CAMBRIDGE
UNIVERSITY PRESS

University Printing House, Cambridge CB2 8BS, United Kingdom

Cambridge University Press is part of the University of Cambridge.

It furthers the University's mission by disseminating knowledge in the pursuit of
education, learning and research at the highest international levels of excellence.

www.cambridge.org
Information on this title: www.cambridge.org/9781107497658

First published 1936
First paperback edition 2015

A catalogue record for this publication is available from the British Library

ISBN 978-1-107-49765-8 Paperback

CONTENTS

v

PREFACE

During the past forty years of a fairly strenuous classical life, it has often occurred to me that Lucretius deserved a book to himself, as much as Catullus, Virgil and Horace, all of whom have more or less recently received the undivided attention of English scholarship. Lucretius alone has had to wait since 1909, when John Masson published a second volume on him as *Epicurean and Poet*. The present book has been planned—and, I hope, executed—on different lines. The reader will find that I have said comparatively little on the details of Atomism, ancient and modern, and have preferred to concentrate on the more human side of Lucretius as poet.[1] A knowledge of Epicurean atoms is easily accessible from the many books which deal with the subject, notably by Dr Cyril Bailey, to whose scholarly and sympathetic treatment of Epicurus I owe a great deal of gratitude, as will be apparent from frequent acknowledgement in my own work. In this I have mainly dealt with the actual achievements of Lucretius as poet—his attitude towards religion and ethics, his anthropology and social science,

[1] I have also omitted other subjects more or less germane to Lucretius, such as his influence later, on which see G. D. Hadzsits, *Lucretius and his Influence*, 1935.

his view of human nature as dependent on the Nature of the Universe. For the sake of completeness, I have often found it necessary to "crib" from my own published books, which indeed were mainly conceived in the hope of a comprehensive work on the great Roman poet. To some extent, my model has been the old, but still invaluable study of Lucretius by Martha, whose *Poëme de Lucrèce* gladdened my undergraduate days.

A few words must be added on the subject of English verse-translations. Formerly, I tried various metres, to represent the *De Rerum Natura*, but am now convinced that, while no metre can do absolute justice to Lucretius, some, at least, of his characteristics can best be preserved in a free treatment of English "heroic" verse. Lucretius is, before all things, a traditionalist; and only the traditional metre used, in different ways, by Milton and Keats, Wordsworth and Coleridge—I ought to add Tennyson's *Lucretius*—can satisfy the Anglo-Saxon ear. None the less, there is much to be said for the Spenserian stanza, which Mr Foxley has recently chosen with such decided success, in his fine translation of the poet.

Lucretius, again, is an archaist; but, in this respect, I have rarely ventured to follow him. Roman literature moved easily and naturally, in the words and forms of bygone generations; but, in English, a "Wardour Street" diction puzzles, if it does not annoy, the average modern reader.

In the Appendix, there will be found some versions of Wordsworth and Matthew Arnold into Lucretian hexameters. My apology for these is the reminder of a classical friend that Latin verse composition—otherwise largely demoded—is a form of criticism, even if there may be few to share my belief that both these poets (especially Wordsworth) have some points in common with Lucretius. Anyhow, the poet himself—as he tells us—wrote for his own Pleasure, as well as for that of others; and a critic, who tries to follow him *non passibus aequis*, may be pardoned for a few *opera*

conquisita diu, dulcique reperta labore.

It remains to acknowledge the assistance of my son, J. G. Sikes, of Jesus College, Cambridge, who has not only corrected the proofs, but has helped in making the Index of this book; and to the Staff of the University Press I am grateful for their care in its preparation.

E. E. S.

January 1936

CHAPTER I

THE GENIUS OF LUCRETIUS

I

How far can a poet, without injuring his proper function, be a teacher? The early Greeks assumed that it was not only his right, but his duty to instruct, whether the instruction was theological, or moral, or physical. There was no rival of the poet in any one of these spheres. The Greek priests were concerned with ritual alone, and rarely, if ever, assumed the office of moralist; the philosophers, such as Parmenides and Empedocles, were content to follow the tradition of Hesiod, who had written verse simply because prose had not been invented. At the very end of the fifth century Aristophanes could still hold that the poet was bound to teach the adult, as the schoolmaster teaches the boy.[1]

But prose was now seriously competing with verse, as the medium for the exposition of philosophy, as well as of history. Aristophanes may have had good reason for his assumption that it was the business of Homer and Aeschylus to teach the manly virtues, but Plato showed that there was an "ancient quarrel" between the poet and the philosopher. His grounds were metaphysical no less

[1] See generally E. E. Sikes, *Greek View of Poetry*.

than moral; and if Aristotle suggested a means of reconciliation, his own definition of the poetic function rigidly excluded philosophy. To Aristotle poetry was concerned with "men in action", and even if human action were interpreted in the most liberal terms, there would be no place for an Empedocles, who was to count as a physicist rather than as a poet. Aristotle's theory was deeply imbued with the ethical purpose of the poet; but he drew a clear line of cleavage between the more or less indirect teaching of morals and the direct exposition of a scientific creed. And, since the days of Aristotle, the breach between science and poetry has, of course, been so enormously widened that any dream of an alliance may well seem impossible. If Atomism is a doubtful and dangerous subject for a Lucretius, no modern poet could conceivably trench on the highly technical ground of the modern physicist. Even for Aristotle Lucretius would have been placed with Empedocles outside the ranks of poets. But Aristotle did not convert his own contemporaries or successors: in the generation after the great philosopher, there was a marked return to the didacticism of Hesiod. The age of Alexander was scientific (according to its lights) and intensely erudite, not to say pedantic. If it was difficult to recapture the spirit of Homer, the learning of Hesiod offered an easier scope for imitation. So, to the Hesiodean subjects of cosmogony and agriculture, the Alexandrians added astronomy and the healing of snake-bites. And Lucretius was Alexandrian, in so far as he followed the didactic method of Aratus, whose *Phaenomena* was admired by other Romans than Cicero. Varro and Germanicus also translated the poem for which Ovid prophesied immortality:

Cum sole et luna semper Aratus erit.

In ancient times, therefore, there was abundant justification for a poem on Nature. The question remains whether modern criticism upholds the judgment. It is not denied that Lucretius was a great poet; but it has been strenuously denied that the *De Rerum Natura* is a poetic subject. A poet —it is often argued—has a reality of his own, and is not directly concerned with the discoveries of science or the logic of philosophy. He must deal, not with the bare facts, but with their appearance and its emotional significance. He may be influenced by his particular theory of the Universe, but it is not his proper business to expound his creed in detail.

There are indeed modern critics who would go further in their objections, by refining poetry to a "purity" which eliminates every trace of the philosophic. According to the school of Mr T. S. Eliot,[1] the original form of philosophy cannot be

[1] *The Sacred Wood*, p. 160 f.

poetic, and Empedocles, being a pioneer, with a
new system to develop, could not approach his
own theories with the detachment proper to a poet.
Lucretius, it is true, takes over a system ready-
made; but, on this view, he too is an innovator,
since he expounds Atomism from start to finish,
leaving no detail to be assumed. If, unlike Empedocles, he may sometimes halt between two different and discordant methods of approach, he
must be classed, for all that really matters, as
Empedoclean.

But the upholders of "pure" poetry claim too
much. To dissociate all serious thought from the
poetic region, to deny that a poet can be an
original thinker, or to confine his proper activity
to "a life of sensation", is the extreme of aestheti-
cism. A few poets, ancient and modern, pass the
test; the majority, with Dante, Milton and Goethe
at their head, follow, more or less closely, a definite
philosophy. Lucretius is surely to be added to their
number, in spite of Coleridge's complaint that
"whatever in Lucretius is poetry is not philosophical, whatever is philosophical is not poetry".[1]
Coleridge must have forgotten the very opening
of the *De Rerum Natura*, when Lucretius trans-

[1] In a letter to Wordsworth. This agrees with the well-known
statement in the *Biographia Literaria* that "a poem is a species
of composition which is opposed to works of science by proposing
for its immediate object pleasure, not truth". But Coleridge also
held that a great poet must be a "profound philosopher".

4

formed the Empedoclean concept of Love and Strife, as the motive power of the Universe, into his magnificent prayer to Venus.[1]

As a Romantic, Coleridge was out of sympathy with didacticism; and, even if we agree that philosophy is a fitting subject for poetic treatment, there is still an objection to the didactic *manner*. This objection, as we have seen, was not valid in classical times, except for Plato; and there cannot be many, at the present time, who would "prefer to be wrong with Plato than right with the others". The Alexandrian Eratosthenes protested that poetry was concerned merely with Delight or Transport, not with Teaching, but the other critics disagreed; Virgil, in his *Georgics*, and even Ovid, in *The Art of Love*, were in the full Alexandrine current.

There the matter, at least in England, rested until the end of the eighteenth century. Poems like the *Essay on Man* had hitherto presupposed the right of the poet to be didactic. But the question became pressing in the Romantic age. For, although Wordsworth regarded himself as a teacher, Keats, in one of his most famous pronouncements, hated a poet who had "a palpable design" upon his reader. Erasmus Darwin's *Loves of the Plants* was certainly no great advertisement for the theory of Instruction. So, in the nineteenth century, it became common form to call didactic

[1] See below, pp. 117f.

verse an illegitimate cross between science and poetry. De Quincey is a good example of this early Victorian attitude. In his essay on Alexander Pope (1848) he is quite dogmatic. No poetry can have the function of teaching, and he bids us "look at the poem of *Cyder* by Philips, of the *Fleece* by Dyer, or (which is a still weightier example) at the *Georgics* of Virgil", asking whether any of these poets shows "the least anxiety for the correctness of your principles?" We may make De Quincey a present of *Cyder* or the *Fleece*, but the *Georgics* is different, and surely does not support his argument: it satisfies both his requirements—it is "beautiful", as well as "correct".

Anyhow, at the present day, we have ceased to be as positive as De Quincey. We have purged ourselves of certain Romantic theories, and are ready to acknowledge that poetry may teach us, if—in the words of a modern critic—it teaches us in art's way.[1] This, perhaps, is not very helpful, since the question may well be asked, What, precisely, *is* art's way? We may admit (unless we believe in "pure" poetry) that every poem must have some "content", and the highest content is no doubt philosophic; but another recent writer allows that "no one has yet succeeded in marking exactly at what point the philosophy becomes a hindrance in our poetic enjoyment. The uttermost

[1] J. L. Lowes, *Convention and Revolt*, p. 215.

that the most competent critic has been able to say is that the teaching must be indirect, and this, as we all feel, is inadequate".[1]

But is not this harping on indirectness, itself a survival of Romantic prejudice? Virgil, in his *Georgics*, is surely direct enough; but we enjoy that poem, because its teaching is coloured with imagination. Robert Bridges, in his *Testament of Beauty*, is frankly, though less obtrusively, as didactic as Lucretius, for whose downright method he substitutes a manner suggesting that he is a learner rather than a teacher. There is little real difference, however, between the technical language of the Roman and the English poet. No details of Atomism, as expounded by Lucretius, are, in themselves, less "poetic" than such lines as

> It was no flaw
> in Leibniz to endow his monad-atoms with mind.

Formally, such statements are pure prose; but they are to be judged not in themselves, but in relation to the whole poem of which they are a part. Coleridge warned us that a poem of any length neither can be, nor ought to be, all poetry; in the same way, Poe explained that a long poem must consist of flat passages interwoven with a series of inspired moments; and, before him, Dryden had pointed to the flats among the elevations of Milton. From

[1] E. E. Kellett, *Fashion in Literature*, p. 249.

Homer onwards, the need of relaxing the tension in poetry, at its highest, has been always recognised. What is true for Homer and Virgil, Sophocles and Shakespeare, must also be true for Lucretius. But, it may be objected, the passages of low emotional power are too numerous in the *De Rerum Natura* to be compared with analogies in (say) Dante or Milton. These poets work essentially in the grand manner, with but occasional excursions into the paths of prose. In Lucretius (it is argued) the proportions are reversed: Atomism bulks too largely: the Greek atom—which to Lucretius, as to Newton, is "matter in solid, massy, hard, impenetrable particles"—cannot be broken by any violence, least of all the violence of the Muses; there are too many desert tracts in the poem where Pegasus is not only pedestrian, but sinks deep in the sands. In this desert, the famous "purple patches" may be oases, but they are all too few. To drop metaphors, Poetry must begin where Science ends.

Such is a common, though not very instructed criticism of the *De Rerum Natura*; and if this were the conclusion of the whole matter, we should be forced to admit that Lucretius, as Quintilian said of Ovid, is only *laudandus in partibus*. If, however, we hold that poetry is not to be confined to mere emotion, but can find room for reason—provided that the intellectual faculty is not too predominant —we can put up a much better defence for the

8

De Rerum Natura. To begin with, we may boldly ask whether reason itself is always unpoetic.[1] "*Nil igitur mors est*": how much of the poetic force of these passionate words is not owed to *igitur* and its implications? Such is the pertinent question of a writer who argues that philosophic poetry, though rare, is to be recognised: if the *Essay on Man* is unsuccessful, Pope's failure was simply due to a lack of interest in his own philosophy.[2]

Perhaps Lucretius, whose avowed object was to please as well as to teach, might have pleased his modern—and even his ancient—readers more if he had tried to teach them less. After all, there was no lack of Epicurean prose-writers or lecturers in Rome—Amafinius and Rabirius in the Latin language, Phaedrus and Philodemus in the Greek. But would any one of these professors have dealt with Atomism like the poet? It is not merely that Lucretius waxes enthusiastic over his physics— enthusiasm, though valuable for a preacher or lecturer, is not the whole equipment for a poet whose mission is to transform scientific fact into human experience. Commentators, who find "arid wastes

[1] The argument here suggested of course runs counter to the usual ideas of poetry; see for example I. A. Richards, *Science and Poetry* (1926), p. 58, "Except occasionally and by accident, logic does not enter at all" (into the poetic approach).

[2] *Times Lit. Suppl.* Aug. 10, 1933. The *igitur* is in a legal argument, enforcing the truth of philosophical poetry; see ch. VII, p. 129.

of dry argument",[1] fail to see the real nature of this argument. The poem is an epic whose hero is not so much Epicurus as Man; and the atoms from which Man is formed are not only significant as the prime elements of the Universe. Although senseless themselves, they contain, in their wonderful changes and interactions, the promise and potency of all Life—human as well as animal and vegetable:

The rain wastes away, when the Heaven-Father has tossed it into the lap of Mother Earth. But shining crops arise, and boughs are green on the trees which grow and bear fruit of themselves. Thence comes nourishment for the race of men and beasts; thence we see cities flourishing with children, and leafy woods singing with a new brood of birds.[2]

And this passage, early in the First book, might well be the text of the whole poem. Even in its most argumentative parts, Lucretius views the atoms in terms of life. His word to describe their combinations is *concilium*, which, as Masson saw, "is most unusual to denote things without life... apparently it must have conveyed to a Roman ear the meaning of 'an assemblage' of living beings".[3] Masson did not pursue this fertile subject; but a later scholar has shown that such Lucretian metaphors are largely drawn, not only from life in

---

[1] The words are from Merrill's edition, p. 43.
[2] I. 250.
[3] Masson, *Lucretius*, vol. I, p. 126.

general, but from the main activities of Roman life in particular.[1] Aristotle had declared that, for a poet, "by far the greatest thing is to be metaphorical",[2] and modern critics mostly agree with him, although the precise value or necessity of the metaphorical may be open to doubt. Coleridge, for example, made qualifications: "images", he said, "however beautiful...do not of themselves characterise the poet"—they must be due to a predominant passion, or when a human and intellectual life is transferred to them from the poet's own spirit. The same note of spirituality is also struck by Mr Middleton Murry: in poetry, metaphor is chiefly a means to excite in us a vague and heightened awareness of qualities which we can best call spiritual.[3]

Whether (with Aristotle) we regard the metaphorical as a mark of genius, or (with later classical writers) as attached to the sphere of art—and really it belongs to both categories—we may profitably linger on this important aspect of Lucretius. He will be found to be among that company of whom Shelley wrote "the language of poets is vitally metaphorical". We might start with the Borgian *Life* of the poet, which gives the interesting

[1] H. S. Davies in the *Criterion*, Oct. 1931. This article on metaphors breaks fresh critical ground.

[2] *Poet.* 1459 *a* 5. In his work περὶ ποιητῶν (fr. 70) Aristotle calls Empedocles "Homeric", partly as being metaphorical.

[3] *Countries of the Mind* (2nd series), p. 7.

story that Lucretius showed his poems to Cicero, who advised him to use metaphors with discretion. Unfortunately this *Life* is now generally recognised as a humanistic invention, so that its evidence has no value, except possibly to show that, in Renascence if not ancient times, the metaphors in the *De Rerum Natura* were already noticed. Many of these, indeed, leap to the eye. We cannot miss his brilliant pictorial description of Religion visualised as a ghoulish demon lowering over mortals with a terrible head, until defeated by Epicurus—a historical Perseus or St George—who returns in triumph, like a Roman consul with his *spolia*, to bring news of victory—*nos exaequat victoria caelo*.[1] Equally visual is the picture of Death—*leti sub dentibus ipsis*[2]—which may well have been prompted by Graeco-Etruscan representations of Charon (Charun), whose grim visage was familiar in Roman gladiatorial shows, as well as in Tuscan art.

But Lucretius by no means confines his metaphors to the visualised image. Some of his concepts are purely mental, such as the famous line

vitaque mancipio nulli datur, omnibus usu.

[1] i. 62 f.

[2] i. 852. For reference to pictures of ghosts cf. iii. 628. The representation of tortures in hell is attested by Plautus, and cf. Cic. *Tusc.* i. 11. See below, p. 127. Horrible teeth are a prominent feature of Charun, the Etruscan messenger of death though not usually the tormentor of the damned, who was Tuchulcha.

Consciously or unconsciously, he followed the Aristotelian preference for metaphors which compared the lifeless with the living—one of the great critic's most profound and most misunderstood contributions to the study of poetry. It has been denied that a poet can be confined to a sphere directly, or even indirectly, concerned with humanity, and the very subject of Lucretius—the Nature of *Things*— has been instanced as a proof that the inanimate is as proper a material for the poet's art as human affairs. A warm admirer of Lucretius remarks on Goethe's *Metamorphosis of Plants* as broadening the bounds of the poetic capacity, and reminds us of Wordsworth's great saying: "poetry is the impassioned expression which is the countenance of all science".[1] But Herford rightly lays stress on *impassioned*, an important qualification: Wordsworth was not moved by Nature in itself, but because he found in Nature something that answered to spiritual needs of his own. Lucretius had no Wordsworthian conception of the natural world; but he knew that what is lifeless is poetically outside the range of human interest, unless his poem made a constant appeal to the heart, as well as to the head. A lesser poet like Aratus, working on strictly didactic lines, appears to have largely

[1] C. H. Herford, *The Poetry of Lucretius* (Bulletin of the John Rylands Library, IV. 2). Reprinted 1918, p. 6 f. Goethe's poems *Die Metamorphose der Pflanzen* and *der Tiere* are part of *Gott und Welt*.

neglected this truth. That astronomer may have hitched his wagon to a star, but he rarely, if ever, brought the star down to human tracks on earth.

The Second book of the *De Rerum Natura* is full of metaphors in which Lucretius seems to forget, for the moment, that his atoms are senseless, and describes their movements by illustrations drawn from the sphere of sentiency and vitality. Thus, the clashing of atoms in the void is shown by the observation that when the sunlight is admitted into a dark room, multitudes of minute bodies are to be seen warring, fighting in squadrons (*turmatim*) with eternal conflict.[1] Even when his proofs of some atomic detail are not drawn, at first hand, from life, the poet turns most readily to the warmth of the living world: the speed of atoms is shown by the analogy of light, "when Aurora sheds new brilliance on lands, and varied birds, flitting in the trackless glades through the yielding air, fill the region with liquid song".[2] So, again, atoms are ever in motion—even when they form the hardest body—since the movements of particles, themselves invisible, must escape the human eye, especially as at a distance visible things appear motionless; sheep, on the hillside, move, and lambs playfully butt; but from afar we see them blended, as a white spot on a green hill.[3] This illustration is immediately followed by the analogy of a fact

[1] ii. 114.   [2] ii. 144.   [3] ii. 308.

which Lucretius must often have observed—"the mimicry of war", "when the plains are filled with the tramp of Roman legions and the cavalry wheel round them; and yet, from some high mountain, all this movement is merged into the appearance of a bright spot resting on the plain":

> *et tamen est quidam locus altis montibus unde*
> *stare videntur et in campis consistere fulgor.*[1]

It would appear, indeed, that the difficulty of his subject had put Lucretius on his mettle: paradoxical as it may seem, there is as much poetry in the Second book, which is largely argumentative, as in any other part of the *De Rerum Natura*. Here the poet was helped by the defects of ancient science, which, as is well known, was content with few observations hardly supported by experiment. Hence it was possible for Lucretius to satisfy the claims of the Graeco-Roman scientist by one or two observations of Nature. It does not much matter whether these were original or drawn from Epicurean manuals; the point is that they are all treated poetically. Thus, differences in the structure of atoms are explained by the observed fact that no two creatures in the whole realm of Nature are exactly alike: the cow knows and misses her calf, sacrificed on the altar; and, as she wanders desolate through the green sward, she recognises

[1] ii. 323; cf. 40 f.

his hoof-prints, "looking everywhere, if perchance she may have sight of her lost offspring, and she stops to fill the leafy woodland with her complaints, and often returns to her byre, smitten with yearning for her calf".[1] This long illustration is immediately followed by a shorter but equally poetic description of the sea-shells, which, in their variety, "paint the bosom of earth where the sea laves the thirsty sand of the curven shore with gentle waves":

> *concharumque genus parili ratione videmus*
> *pingere telluris gremium, qua mollibus undis*
> *litoris incurvi bibulam pavit aequor harenam.*[2]

The lines have often been quoted as examples of the poet's fine observation; they are even more remarkable, perhaps, for the gem-like beauty of the expression, which shows that Lucretius could add to his qualities of force and dignity, the haunting charm and delicacy of Catullus, who might well have composed the little passage. These examples have all been chosen from a single book, to prove that, in the most technical part of his work, Lucretius never, for long, forgets his mission to "teach delightfully". It would, indeed, be easy to instance the most striking features of his genius from this book alone, which might almost serve as a kind of compendium for the Epicurean creed, to be expanded in the following books. Its proem strikes the note of morality, clearly showing the

[1] ii. 355 f.   [2] ii. 374.

definition of Pleasure as the negation of Pain; and
even an English translation may preserve something of its uncompromising directness:

> 'Tis sweet, when the rough sea is tempest-tost,
> Safe upon land, to mark another's toil:
> Not that the sight of one in dire distress
> Gives pleasure, but 'tis sweet to contemplate
> Ills thou thyself art spared; and sweet, to view
> Great armies marshalled in the battle-field,
> And take no part therein; but joy of joys,
> To hold the peaceful citadel of the Wise,
> Builded by knowledge and impregnable.
> Therefrom thou mayest look down and see the herd
> Who seek astray some devious path of life,
> At random. Emulous in wit, in rank,
> They climb and struggle, contending night and day
> For wealth and power. O miserable minds!
> O purblind hearts! How dark the way ye tread,
> How perilous, when your petty span of life
> Stumbles in error! Are ye so ignorant
> Of Nature, who proclaims, for all to hear,
> Her only need—a body untouched by pain,
> That, free from care and all disquietude,
> The mind may gain fruition of sweet sense?[1]

In the same book, too, we learn his deductions
from the general theory of atoms, as seen both in
the material world and in human life. The earth,
being formed of atoms in perpetual warfare, cannot persist for ever. For a time it is held together
by "isonomy"—the equal forces of destruction
and preservation, which gain the mastery in alter-

[1] ii. 1–19.

nate sequence, just as in human generations the
crying of the infant at birth is mingled every day
with lamentation for the dead;[1] but, in the end,
our world is doomed; for though she contains all
the seeds which form land and water, with all
things living, she cannot be called divine, as the
ancient Greek poets falsely imagined. And here
Lucretius finds occasion to describe the procession
in honour of the Great Mother, borne through
cities in a car with her armed Phrygian priests as
attendants, while the crowd of worshippers strew
all her path with coins, and cover the image with
the snow of roses—*ninguntque rosarum floribus um-
brantes Matrem comitumque catervas*.[2] But this is mere
ignorance: the gods need no gifts, and are self-
sufficient, with no thought of man—*nec bene pro-
meritis capitur neque tangitur ira*—so that to call the
whole earth Mother (as the sea is called Neptune
and the crops Ceres) is only lawful, if the mind is
kept free of foul superstition.

The place of these departmental gods was partly
filled by the quasi-personification of Nature. As a
philosophical concept, the *De Rerum Natura* in Lucretius is hardly developed from the *Physis* by which
Empedocles described the sum-total of existing
things. To the Roman poet, as to the Greek,
Nature is often merely this *rerum summa, omne quod
est*, a non-sentient collection of atoms that form

[1] ii. 569–580; cf. ii. 1144 f.   [2] ii. 600 f.

the material of the Universe. But the parts of this Whole act and interact by the operation of certain laws—*foedera naturai*—inherent in the constitution of matter. Such "laws" need not, of course, imply the existence of a personal law-giver; but although Lucretius is quite sound on the first principle of his creed, strenuously denying all sentiency and purpose in his creative atoms, he seems none the less apt to endow Nature with the will and power of a personal creator—*rerum natura creatrix*. In this mood he can identify her with Venus, at the opening of his poem. Sometimes, it is true, the poet holds to his strict philosophy, remembering that Nature, after all, is composed of senseless atoms; but, even so, he appears to halt between the poetical and the Epicurean approach, as when his Nature— "if she had utterance"—would want to raise her voice in reproof of the man who recoils from death.

It is this side of Lucretius that the great French critic, Patin, emphasised in the pregnant phrase *l'anti-Lucrèce chez Lucrèce*.[1] Writing as a Catholic for Catholics, he drew attention to the poet's unconscious inconsistency, and pointed out that his conception of *rerum natura gubernans* really implied the existence of a Deity, both sentient and powerful, who had created the world, and governed it providentially. There can be no doubt that many expressions in the *De Rerum Natura* may be so inter-

[1] M. Patin, *Études sur la poésie latine*, ch. vII.

preted; but it might be argued that this attitude
is not so much theological as poetic. Lucretius was
perfectly satisfied with his *religion*, which must have
seemed to him to be a vast improvement on older
polytheism;[1] but, as a poet, he regretted the loss
of the Myth, so inextricably bound up with the
Greek mode of poetic expression. This hostility,
not only to Greek religion but to the traditional
mode of its expression, marks Lucretius as a solitary
soul, in literature as well as in philosophy. Unlike
his predecessors in the Scipionic circle, his contemporaries the Neoterics, and the Augustans, he belonged to no clique, and set no fashion to follow.[2]

Lucretius interprets an era in which the poet
has lost belief in

The fair humanities of old religion[3]

and can no longer employ these humanities to serve
his poetic need. Much later, Lucan represented
another such age, but his compensation for the loss
of the Myth was a plentiful use of superstition,
which suited both the Stoic poet and his audience.
Poetry had to choose between the old well-worn
path, to which it had so long been accustomed,

[1] See below, ch. VI.

[2] The Stoic Manilius is perhaps an exception to this statement.
His *Astronomica* (written about the end of the Augustan age) is
a belated answer to the *De Rerum Natura*. On the solitariness of
Lucretius see O. Regenbogen, *Lucrez* (Leipzig, 1932), p. 15 f.:
"Lucrez ist allein".

[3] S. T. Coleridge (after Schiller).

20

and a new untried avenue; and it is little wonder
that at this crisis the poets should often have turned
wistful glances backward, lamenting, like Wordsworth, the lapse of a creed outworn. Wordsworth,
indeed, had at first tried to compromise; but his
classical experiment—*Laodamia*—must have proved
that there comes a time when poetry can no longer
be forced into traditional modes of thought. Lucretius, it is true, was in a different position from the
English poet, who did not believe that Laodamia
had ever existed; to the Roman, Iphigenia was a
very real victim of religion, and there is, of course,
a vast gulf between a mere poetic convention and
a serious religious belief (or disbelief). None the
less, Lucretius obviously resented, as a poet, the
loss of the Myth; and he did his utmost to preserve
it, even at the cost of some violence to his philosophy, as is at once apparent in the opening prayer
to Venus. That invocation, indeed, requires to be
very specially explained;[1] for, in it, Lucretius
seems not only to be staining his own mind with
foul superstition (by the mere mention of Venus
and Mars), but actually makes a supplication to
the goddess who, as his creed insisted, could neither
hear nor answer his prayer.

Apart from the address to Venus, however, there
are numerous passages, scattered about the poem,
which show how clearly Lucretius clung to the

[1] See below, p. 117 for a full discussion of the Invocation.

myths, even if he were hardly conscious of their
poetic content. We have seen that the myth and
ritual of the Earth-goddess inspired him to one of
his finest descriptions; and his beautiful account
of Mother Earth fructified by Heaven, the All-
Father,[1] is another example, among many, of the
use to which the old religion could be turned,
without prejudice to the new materialism. Again,
he argues that there is no such monster as a goat-
foot Satyr or a half-bestial Pan.[2] But Lucretius
depicts them, as any mythological poet might do,
even while condemning the credulity of those who
believe in such superstitions. The word "depict"
is used advisedly; for, in the beautiful account of
the seasons—the procession of Spring, with Venus
and her winged boy, the Zephyr and Flora; of
Summer, attended by Ceres; and of the other
seasons in turn—Lucretius seems to have been inspired (like Catullus in his *Peleus and Thetis*) by
some Greek frieze or tapestry.[3] To the philosopher,
Greek myths were worse than useless; but Lucretius
was more than a philosopher; and he must have
shared the yearning, so well expressed by a modern
poet:

---

[1] ii. 991 f. The lines are an echo of Aeschylus (fr. 44) describing
the love of Heaven and Earth; cf. also Eur. *Chrysippus* (fr. 839).

[2] iv. 580 f.

[3] v. 737 f. On poetic descriptions of works of art see A. L.
Wheeler, *Catullus*, p. 133 f.

The words of Arcady are dead,
And over is their antique joy;
Of old the world on dreaming fed;
Grey truth is now her painted toy;
Yet still she turns her restless head.[1]

So Coleridge, in the translation from Schiller which has just been quoted, had complained that poets paid dearly for the loss of the Fable:

But still the heart doth need a language, still
Doth the old instinct bring back the old names.

And Lucretius has given us more than a hint that he belongs to the company of Wordsworth, Coleridge and Yeats.

With Wordsworth, indeed, the Roman poet has other qualities in common. A comparison between the two poets may seem paradoxical if not ludicrous. They might appear to be poles apart—Wordsworth a pantheist; Lucretius, practically, if not philosophically, an atheist. Both, again, started with Nature, though she taught each a very different lesson. But poetry is the expression of an attitude, not a mere matter of creed. Lucretius shares with Wordsworth an earnestness of purpose, a striving to get at the root of things, an enthusiasm for the truth, a burning desire that his poetry should be moral, in the sense that there is morality in every great poem.

It is surely in recognition of this likeness that a

[1] Yeats, *The Song of the Happy Shepherd*.

modern practitioner of Latin verse is almost forced
to choose the Lucretian, rather than the Virgilian
model, in order to express the more adequately the
spirit which informed Wordsworth at his highest.[1]
No doubt this sublimity is not a prerogative of the
poet who wrote *The world is too much with us*;
Matthew Arnold, whose definition of "high serious-
ness" would suit both Lucretius and Wordsworth,
as well as Homer and Dante, can himself exhibit a
vein of the sublime, and may sometimes deserve the
honour of suggesting the hexameters of the *De Rerum
Natura*; but Arnold is too Stoic to be often remi-
niscent of the Epicurean poet—even when the
Epicurean was most Stoic—and the characteristic
Dover Beach strikes anything but a Lucretian note.

There are some who object to all comparisons
between poets, and they have good reason: a great
poet should be treated as unique. Wordsworth
himself might not have felt complimented by being
compared with even so renowned a name as Lucretius. Yet a poet, if unique, also belongs to a class
whose members have many characteristics in common; otherwise they would not be poets at all;
and it is not wonderful that the Roman and the
English teacher, who both learned their lessons
from Nature, should have taught with the same

---

[1] It must be noted, however, that *Tintern Abbey* is essentially
Virgilian; cf. *Georg.* iv. 219 f. with *A sense sublime*.... Both passages
are pantheistic.

spirit, even if the lessons themselves were so different as to supply a contrast rather than a comparison.

II

So far, Lucretius has been discussed mainly in connection with the minuteness of atoms; but he is telescopic as well as microscopic. Wordsworth might well have been thinking of the *De Rerum Natura* when he wrote of the man

> Who hath among least things
> An under-sense of greatest; sees the parts
> As parts, but with a feeling of the whole.

Even if our Universe is doomed to destruction, he yields to no poet in his admiration for the majesty of Nature—*maiestas cognita rerum*. A small poet, indeed, would hardly have chosen the most stupendous of all subjects. Dante and Milton showed their greatness by the conception, as well as the execution of their epics. But Lucretius has a very special claim to be called great. No Epicurean, least of all Epicurus himself, had hitherto seen the poetic, as distinct from the philosophic significance of his system. What the founder of the school thought of poetry and of literature in general may be gathered from his advice "to sail past it with stopped ears, as from the Sirens' song".[1] From

[1] Fr. Epicur. v. 33 Bailey. On the lack of Greek Epicurean poetry, see my *Roman Poetry*, p. 160 f.

the standpoint of philosophy he had reason enough. Poetry was too much concerned with emotion, which it was the business of the philosopher to suppress; too much bound up with the myths, so that, as we have seen, even Lucretius found it difficult to steer clear of those Sirens. His contemporary, Cicero, remarked on the insensibility of most Epicureans to literature.[1]

Epicurus himself—to judge from his writings—was strangely incapable of realising the beauty and grandeur of the Universe, his mind being fixed, not on the flaming walls of the world, but on the problem of man's conduct, unguided by the gods. He claimed to find his peace mainly in the constant investigation of Nature;[2] but his extant writings nowhere suggest any poetic inspiration drawn from his great subject. It is true that such phenomena as the motion of celestial bodies fill him, like Lucretius, with awe,[3] and he is at pains to preserve their majestic significance (σέμνωμα). Nevertheless, he insists that this awe must never degenerate into superstitious fear,[4] and it is quite unconnected with the pleasure of scientific pursuits. Lucretius,

---

[1] Cic. *Pis.* 29. In Cicero's day, the Epicurean Philodemus wrote a study on poetry; see C. Jensen, *Philodemus über die Gedichte, fünfter Buch* (1923). Lucretius, therefore, was not alone in neglecting his master's distrust of poetry.   [2] Epicur. *Ep.* i. 37.

[3] Lucr. iii. 28: *divina voluptas percipit atque horror.* The *horror* is itself pleasant; cf. Statius, *Theb.* i. 490: *laetusque per artus horror iit.*

[4] Epicur. *Ep.* i. 76 f.

being a poet, as well as an enthusiastic Epicurean, does his master more than justice in a eulogy, the terms of which might more aptly apply to his own genius:

so the living force of his spirit prevailed; he passed far beyond the flaming bulwarks of the world, and traversed in mind and soul the whole immensity; thence returning a conqueror, he brings news of what can, what cannot, come into being, what powers and deep-set boundary-marks are appointed for each thing. Wherefore superstition in her turn is trampled under foot, and victory raises men to heaven.[1]

There is hardly a trace of this enthusiasm to be found in Epicurus. The observation of Nature may be entirely due to the master; but the imaginative treatment is the pupil's own. Epicurus might well be one who, in the words of Lucretius, was *fessus satiate videndi*[2]—wearied with viewing the luminous regions of the sky, which the poet describes in lines of wonderful power:

> *luna, dies, et nox, et noctis signa severa*
> *noctivagaeque faces caeli flammaeque volantes*[3]

a passage which led Bentley to ask whether there was no poetry in "plain vulgar language".[4] Wordsworth, of course, would have agreed with Bentley; but it should here be noted that Lucretius himself, who obtained his poetic effects so largely by archaism, had no particular need for this plain

[1] i. 72 f.   [2] ii. 1038.   [3] v. 1190 f.
[4] *Bentley's Dissertations*, ed. W. Wagner, p. 248.

vulgar language. He knew, however, that the sun was not magnified by calling it "Phoebus".

III

Wordsworth defined a poet as "a man speaking to men: a man, it is true, endued with a more lively sensibility, more enthusiasm and tenderness, who has a greater knowledge of human nature, and a more comprehensive soul than are supposed to be common among mankind". The definition might be illustrated by the genius of Lucretius. His enthusiasm in expounding the details of Atomism has already been mentioned; his sensibility and tenderness are no less characteristic. A sympathy with animals—seen in his reference, already quoted, to the cow yearning for her calf—would mark him as unique among Roman poets, if we did not remember Virgil, whose tears for mortal things must have included the nightingale's lament. But it is by virtue of sympathy with his fellow-men that Lucretius is supreme among Roman poets, Virgil again being excepted. This note of pathos is struck at the very outset of the poem, when—among the evils of superstition—he describes the cruelty of a savage religion, ending in the indignant comment *tantum religio potuit suadere malorum*:

> Herein thou mayest haply shrink, and fear
> Lest thou be impious, entering Reason's school

To tread in sinners' steps. Nay, oftentime
'Tis Superstition that herself has caused
The impious act. Hence came the horrible crime
Whereby the princes, Danaan chivalry,
Slew at the altar of the Huntress-maid
Iphianassa, shameful sacrifice.
The fillets bound about her virginal hair
Dropt equal, covering both her cheeks; she saw
Her wretched father stand on the altar-steps,
She saw the sacrificers at his side
Conceal the knife, while weeping citizens
Gazed; and then, mute for very fearfulness,
She fell; it nought availed her that the king
Had from her first gotten the name of sire.
By rough men was she handled, and shuddering
Brought to the altar, not with escort due
And bridal-song, after the marriage rite,
But haled, a maiden chaste, ripe to be wed,
Victim of her own father, that the fleet
Might win a fair and fortunate voyaging.
—Such crimes could Superstition teach mankind.[1]

In quite a different connection we remember the
poet's famous description of the wife welcoming
her husband home, while his children "hurry to
snatch the first kiss and touch his heart with silent
joy".[2] It is clear, too, from another passage, that
Lucretius attaches great importance to the natural
affection of family life in the history of the human
race, which could not have survived without some
altruism to mitigate the *foedus* or social contract.[3]
These natural instincts the poet freely admits in

[1] i. 80–101. [2] iii. 894 f.
[3] v. 1011–1027. On the social contract, see pp. 154, 166.

lines where womankind, and children, with their inarticulate cries and gestures, prove that "it is right for all men to pity the weak".

Such is Lucretius as poet. In his more philosophic moods, we find him a true Roman satirist. Less lenient than the easy Horace, he has all the force of Juvenal, without raising in our minds the uncomfortable misgiving that Juvenal's *saeva indignatio* may be partly a rhetorical pose. The indignation of Lucretius is certainly not due to rhetoric, for, although he may be rhetorical,[1] he belonged to a generation too early to be corrupted, like Ovid and the post-Augustans, with the worst features of that blot on Latin poetry; nor is it a pose; his earnestness and sincerity are apparent in every page of the *De Rerum Natura*. Like a true disciple of his master, he preaches contentment with a little—*neque enim est umquam penuria parvi*—and castigates the folly and danger of ambition. But he seems to rise above the commonplaces of Epicurean diatribe in his satiric observations of life. Many of such lines or passages linger in the memory: notably, his vivid description of aristocratic boredom, when a Roman noble, "to escape himself, drives furiously from his town-house to his villa, as though hastening to save a burning roof, and then, as soon as he has reached the door, either yawns and seeks relief in sleep, or hurries back to

[1] See ch. vii, p. 136.

30

Rome".[1] The passage moved Arnold to a fine imitation, which gives the spirit of the original:

> In his cool hall, with haggard eyes,
> The Roman noble lay;
> He drove abroad, in furious guise,
> Along the Appian Way.
> He made a feast, drank fierce and fast
> And crown'd his head with flowers—
> No easier nor no happier pass'd
> The impracticable hours.[2]

Lucretius is equally a satirist in his treatment of sexual passion, of which Epicurus had said that it never did a man good, and he is lucky if it has done him no harm.[3] The poet was not a Galahad or a puritan, but his description of a man in the toils of "love" cannot be matched in the whole range of Latin poetry.[4] No aspect of sexual passion is omitted or glozed over; yet the whole description leaves no bad taste in the reader's mouth. There is nothing of Ovid's lubricity or of Juvenal's grossness. Here, as elsewhere, the poet is intensely serious, and sounds the note of the Hebrew Preacher: *Vanity of Vanities.* In vain does the lover try to please his mistress with gifts of cloaks and dresses, perfumes and jewels and chaplets—in vain, "be-

---

[1] iii. 1060 f.   [2] *Obermann once more.*
[3] Diog. L. x. 118; Bailey, *Epicurus*, p. 122, 8.
[4] iv. 1058–1287. The treatment of sexual passion naturally follows the more general discussion on the senses.

cause from the midmost fountain of his bliss a
bitterness comes to poison the very flowers":

> *nequidquam, quoniam medio de fonte leporum*
> *surgit amari aliquid, quod in ipsis floribus angat.*[1]

The bitterness, Lucretius explains, may lie in an
uneasy conscience—even an Epicurean could feel
the pricks of conscience for idleness or immorality[2]
—or the course of this untrue love may not be
smoothed by jealousy: a mistress may utter some
chance word to rankle in the lover's heart, or he
may think that she casts flirting glances at some
other man, with "the vestige of a scornful smile"
at himself. There is much more. Lucretius is deter-
mined to omit no argument in this *Remedium
Amoris*. There is the curious passage about the language of lovers, which seems to suggest the experiences of an Ovid without his erotic purpose;[3]
and there is the final fling at the lover's passion,
and his disgust at the mistress who tries to conceal
what goes on behind the scenes of life—*vitae post-
scaenia.*[4]

Those who search for anything that may be
called specifically Platonic or Romantic in this
attitude will be disappointed. There is nothing to
suggest that Lucretius knew the *Symposium*; but,
if he had read Plato (as he may well have done),

[1] iv. 1133.
[2] On the conscience see p. 128.
[3] iv. 1160–1169.
[4] iv. 1170–1191.

he would certainly have disagreed with the idealisa-
tion of Love and Beauty. Passion, for Lucretius,
is very far removed from the affection of family
life to which he elsewhere refers as one of the main
pleasures that death must interrupt.[1] In his respect
for *coniugibus nostris* he is a true Roman, no mere
follower of his Master, who had counselled the wise
man to marry and have children.[2] With this side
of Roman life, however, Lucretius is little concerned: there is, in fact, no proof that he was ever
married. In the Fourth book his main concern
is to explain the physiology of "love", although
this aspect naturally leads to moralising. Here, of
course, he is no *Epicuri de grege porcus*, but he does
not rise superior to the limitations of ancient sexual
morality. As well summed up by Sellar,[3] it is not
the need of greater purity, but the need of greater
strength that he enforces. His main quarrel is with
the absorbing interest in "love" to which the
young aristocrats, like Catullus, were easy victims.
So far, he is a true Epicurean. Sexual passion,
indeed, was not sent *divinitus*; the myth of Phaedra
and Hippolytus, driven to their destruction by the
compelling power of Venus, would have seemed as

---

[1] iii. 894 f. Cf. iv. 1277.

[2] Diog. L. x. 119. In face of this definite statement, the contrary
evidence of Clemens Alexandrinus (Usener, 526) must be disregarded. But Epicurus did not follow his own advice.

[3] *Roman Poets of the Republic*, p. 303 f.

foolish as the tale of Iphigenia—his classical instance of religious cruelty. But, if passion was
natural, Nature must be curbed by the philosopher.
On this point, all the schools agreed. Even the
Cyrenaic Aristippus prided himself on his self-
sufficiency,[1] while Cynics and Stoics were equally
insistent on the virtue—not of abstinence, but of
moderation. The motto of *nequid nimis* may satisfy
that facile Epicurean, Horace;[2] it is quite inadequate for Lucretius, whose sincerity of purpose is
nowhere—except in his protests against superstition—more eloquent than in his fervid advocacy
of Restraint. The main argument of the schools—
the loss of independence—

adde quod alterius sub nutu degitur aetas[3]

is, for him, only one out of the *mala innumerabilia*
arising from passion unrestrained; and, even if we
feel that his premisses are one-sided, we must recognise the firmness of his convictions and the nobility
of their expression. If Lucretius is not Romantic,
he is at least a Roman, carrying on the tradition
of Cato.

[1] As in his boast ἔχω Λαΐδα, ἀλλ' οὐκ ἔχουαι (Diog. L. ii. 8. 74).
[2] See especially Hor. *Sat.* i. 2.
[3] iv. 1122.

CHAPTER II

THE ART OF LUCRETIUS

I

Modern critics are distinctly shy of discussing the art of Lucretius, and prefer to concentrate on his genius. In a sense they are right, for we have learned that the sharp distinction, drawn by ancient critics between the two phases of poetry, is really invalid. If a poet has "genius", that quality will find expression in appropriate "art". As Horace knew, the pair are not to be separated—they are sworn friends. Nevertheless, Horace, like all ancient critics, thought that these "friends" were separate qualities which could be distinguished, whereas, to the modern, they are, at most, two sides of the same coin. The work of Lucretius itself will serve as an example of their union. Arnold's method of judging good poetry, by single lines or short passages, hardly commends itself at the present day as an infallible test; it must logically lead to the condemnation of a poet by his worst lines—a procedure which Wordsworth and Tennyson would scarcely survive.[1] But Arnold's "touchstones" will

---

[1] The converse equally holds good: Burgon's famous line—"A rose-red city half as old as Time"—was a brilliant inspiration, but it did not redeem his poem from mediocrity.

at least illustrate the difficulty of deciding between the conflicting claims of genius and art. Take any of the great Lucretian verses:

> *nil igitur mors est ad nos, neque pertinet hilum,*

or the passage beginning

> *iam iam non domus accipiet te laeta neque uxor optima....*

Where, it may well be asked, does Genius end here, and Art begin? Both are present, but fused beyond chemical separation. In the modern jargon, there is a single intuition, a perfect concept perfectly expressed. Yet, the old antithesis has a value, if only for convenience' sake. Classical critics did a service (if rather an obvious one) to the study of literature by contrasting the rough *ingenium* of Ennius and the sophisticated *ars* of Callimachus, just as the Victorian critics distinguished between the "rugged style" of Browning and the Alexandrian polish of Tennyson. The Graeco-Romans no doubt laid too much stress on Form, because genius cannot be defined or analysed, whereas the beauties of art could be easily recognised. "Execution", said Blake, "is the chariot of genius"; but ancient critics too often confused the chariot with the driver.

But Lucretius is himself a great artist, although —as we shall presently see in more detail—his technique is of course not entirely Virgilian; and

36

further there are some features which the ancients, in their clear-cut dichotomy, would regard as artistic, whereas the moderns would see in them examples of natural power. The difference of outlook may be illustrated by the first Roman appreciation of Lucretius, in a correspondence of 54 B.C. between Cicero and his brother. In answer to a letter (now lost) from Quintus, who had apparently discussed the *De Rerum Natura* after the poet's recent death, Marcus wrote: *Lucreti poemata ut scribis ita sunt multis ingeni luminibus multae tamen artis.*[1] The adverb *tamen* long vexed the editors, who tried to insert *non* before either *multis* or *multae*. But the text is now admittedly correct, whatever the significance of the *tamen*. This word may possibly explain *ita*; Cicero, it has been argued, would not repeat Quintus, without adding something of his own. His brother may well have denied art (as defined by the Alexandrians) to Lucretius, and Marcus would say: "You are right about his genius, but I find in him plenty of art as well".[2] There is, however, a simpler explanation: poets, except the very greatest, like Homer and Sophocles, were sharply divided into two classes—those who had *ingenium* and those who only showed art, the possession of both being

[1] *ad Q. fratr.* ii. 9. 3. Punctuation must for the moment be omitted, as prejudging the sense.

[2] See H. W. Litchfield in *Class. Phil.* xxiv (1913).

37

thought very rare.[1] Ennius was refused artistic merit by Ovid:

Ennius ingenio maximus, arte rudis,

just as Longinus denied genius to some of the Alexandrines.[2] But Statius seems to allow the double honour to Lucretius: *et docti furor arduus Lucreti*, where *furor* refers to genius, *docti* to art; and Cicero may have paid the poet a great compliment in linking him with the highest, who could combine both qualities, thought to be almost mutually exclusive.[3]

Even so, a difficulty remains: what precisely does Cicero understand by the *lumina ingeni*? The accepted rendering is "flashes", which is certainly wrong. Elsewhere Cicero uses the plural of this word, not for intermittent gleams, but for high lights, brilliances, especially in connection with the Figures (σχήματα λέξεως καὶ διανοίας). For instance, he says that an oration needs plenty of *lumina—quasi luminibus distinguenda et frequentanda omnis oratio sententiarum et verborum.*[4] It is true that, to a modern, these Figures would seem to fall under the category of art; but to Cicero, as to Longinus, their proper *use* is proof of genius. We

[1] With a change of punctuation (a colon after *ita sunt*).

[2] Ovid, *Trist.* ii. 424; Longinus, *De Subl.* 33.

[3] Norden (*Ant. Kunstp.* i. 182 *a* 1), holding this view, compares Seneca, *Contr.* pr. i. 17: *memoria ei natura quidem felix, plurimum tamen arte adiuta.*

[4] *De Orat.* iii. 201; so *Orator*, 67, 83, 134, 181.

need not, however, assume that Cicero would have
limited the genius of Lucretius to the use of the
Figures. He was a warm admirer of Ennius, and
must have approved of the glowing tribute which
Lucretius paid to the founder of Latin poetry.
Lucretius himself, as is well known, had little
sympathy with the Neoterics, the fashionable Roman school derived from Alexandria, of which
Calvus and Catullus were the chief members. It is
not accidental that the most recent account of
Catullus has only casual and unimportant references to his contemporary;[1] except in time, the
two poets had practically nothing in common,
either in style or aim. Cicero's own excursions
into poetry favoured the Ennian tradition; and,
as we have just seen, Ennius was, at least in the
view of the Augustans, a genius, but "rude in
art". The orator, however, did not anticipate
Ovid; the technical improvements made by Lucretius on the rough model of Ennius must have
been pleasing for the sufficient reason that Cicero
himself had pointed the way, since his own early
Aratea certainly influenced the *De Rerum Natura* in
metre and language, although not of course by
inspiration.[2] Apart from these metrical and verbal

[1] *Catullus*, by A. L. Wheeler.

[2] The date of Cicero's *Aratea* may be placed before his journey
to Greece in 79–77 B.C. See W. B. Sedgwick, *Class. Rev.* xxxvii
(1923), p. 115 f. and W. W. Ewbank, *The Poems of Cicero* (1933),
p. 23 f.

improvements, the whole conception and plan of a
didactic poem came under the category of art, and
here Cicero, as the translator of Aratus, was a
competent judge. Lucretius was clearly *doctus*, even
if his *doctrina* was deplorable.

It was, then, as a Roman traditionalist that
Lucretius appealed to Cicero; but Latin poetry
was still young for Cicero, and Roman tradition
was short. In one sense, this did not matter; there
was all Greek poetry to draw on, and Lucretius
starts with the fountain-head. The great description of the Homeric heaven inspired him, as well
as other poets in their turn:

> *apparet divom numen sedesque quietae,*
> *quas neque concutiunt venti nec nubila nimbis*
> *aspergunt neque nix acri concreta pruina*
> *cana cadens violat, semperque innubilus aether*
> *integit, et large diffuso lumine rident.*[1]

The theory and practice of Imitation were so
universally observed in classical times—to survive
through the nineteenth century—that it is no
wonder if the beautiful lines of Homer found
conscious echoes in Tennyson and Swinburne:
Tennyson, in his *Lucretius*, had of course a special

---

[1] iii. 18–22, after Hom. *Od.* vi. 43 f.:

Οὔλυμπόνδ᾽ ὅθι φασὶ θεῶν ἕδος ἀσφαλὲς αἰεὶ
ἔμμεναι· οὔτ᾽ ἀνέμοισι τινάσσεται, οὔτε ποτ᾽ ὄμβρῳ
δεύεται, οὔτε χιὼν ἐπιπίλναται· ἀλλὰ μάλ᾽ αἴθρη
πέπταται ἀνέφελος, λευκὴ δ᾽ ἐπιδέδρομεν αἴγλη·
τῷ ἔνι τέρπονται μάκαρες θεοὶ ἤματα πάντα.

motive for his imitation—"nor ever falls the least
white star of snow"—and the rest. Less familiar,
perhaps, is the splendid passage in the *Atalanta*,
where Swinburne transferred the home of the gods
to a description of Elysium:

> Lands indiscoverable in the unheard-of west
> Round which the strong stream of a sacred sea
> Rolls without wind for ever, and the snow
> There shows not her white wings and windy feet,
> Nor thunder nor swift rain saith anything,
> Nor the sun burns, but all things rest and thrive.

This is Imitation, at its best. There can be no
question of "theft" by Lucretius or the two
English poets; each has preserved his own individuality, though all derive from a single source.
At the present day, Imitation is outmoded, and
the change of fashion is, no doubt, on the whole
for good; but the success of the three passages may
well give pause to the most "original" of modern
poets.[1]

II

Criticism of any author cannot afford to neglect
the views of his own contemporaries, if only because such critics are presumably the most intelligent members of a poet's audience, and best
understand his immediate appeal. If the philosophy of Lucretius cannot be judged without re-

[1] I have discussed Imitation in *The Greek View of Poetry*,
especially on Longinus, p. 233 f.

ference to the ideas of the time, it is quite as necessary to examine the current theories on poetic art. In the age of Lucretius and Cicero the criticism of Theophrastus, the successor of Aristotle, held the field. The main literary activity of the Peripatetic school was directed to a search for the key, or keys, of style; and they found two keys, which seemed to unlock the secrets of literature, whether in poetry or prose: the first was the Choice of words (ἐκλογὴ ὀνομάτων); the second, Order (σύνθεσις), including both the pattern of words and the management of clauses.

With regard to the Choice of words, the most casual reader of Lucretius is at once impressed by his extreme archaism: he rejects the *usus* of his contemporaries—Cicero, in prose, Catullus, in verse—and harks back to Ennius. An archaic diction may no doubt be affected by different poets from various motives—delight in the unfamiliar word or form, the pure joy of writing (as Cicero said) "another language", not vulgarised by common speech. Poets, again, when dealing with the past, will naturally suit their style to the language of the past. But Lucretius, in subject, was mainly concerned with the present or rather, perhaps, with the timeless; and his predominant motive was surely a desire to carry on the form of Roman poetry, in opposition to the new school—to wear the laurel-leaf which consecrated and was con-

42

secrated by the head of Ennius. It is significant, indeed, that in describing this crown he uses archaic language—

per gentes Italas hominum quae clara clueret.[1]

If imitation is the sincerest form of tradition, as well as of flattery, a poet was bound to archaise, when even prose, in the Ciceronian age, was deeply penetrated by old-world diction. Cicero himself, with writers like Cotta and Caelius Rufus, followed in his philosophical writings the normal educated speech of the day;[2] but historians, such as Q. Claudius Quadrigarius and L. Cornelius Sisenna, tried to recapture the style of Cato, if not of the Twelve Tables. Sallust, at the end of the period, is the best known, but by no means the only example of archaising. Style, no less than *mores*, produced the men of whom Ennius had said,

moribus antiquis res stat Romana virisque,

and now Ennius was himself *antiquus*. With much greater reason than the prose-writers, Lucretius falls into line with those who stood on the ancient ways. Apart from tradition (which of course includes much more than the linguistic element) he found in archaic language a valuable ally for his

---

[1] Cf. Ennius:

nostra Latinos
per populos terrasque poemata clara cluebunt.

[2] See J. F. D'Alton, *Roman Literary Theory*, p. 273 f. and the present writer in the *Cambridge Ancient History*, vol. ix, p. 766 f.

poetry. Later Roman poets—Virgil, to some degree, is an exception—used archaism but sparingly. In consequence, the diction of Roman poets approximated to that of prose-writers; and Gray, remarking that "the language of the age is never the language of poetry, except among the French", might have added the Romans, who did no more than refine upon the common speech.[1] The parent Latin, in fact, suffered from the same disability as the French. But Lucretius (whether consciously or unconsciously) solved the problem by the simple expedient of using "another language", as the orator Antonius had properly described poetic diction in his own age.[2]

Lucretius is quite as traditional in his love of alliteration and assonance—both of which seem to go back to the very roots of old Italian as of old English poetry. For, so far from being mere ornaments or adjuncts to poetic charm, the use of both was apparently an effective part of Saturnian poetry, strong enough to resist the influence of Greek verse, which normally disregarded these forms of rhyme. Even Catullus, for all his Graecism, was here thoroughly Italian;[3] and Lucretius is at least as fond of assonance and alliteration as either Ennius or Catullus. Art should conceal art,

[1] I have developed this point in *Roman Poetry*, p. 222 f.
[2] In Cic. *De Orat.* ii. 61.
[3] *Roman Poetry*, ch. VII.

no doubt, and Lucretius may sometimes have over-stepped the mark in his adjustment of sound to meaning. But alliteration and similar so-called "aids" are an element integral to poetry, helping to control the passion that might otherwise gain the upper hand, and so mar the symmetry of an organic work of art.[1]

These varieties of rhyme have often been re-garded as "characteristic of an immature, and not of a finished literature".[2] For the "finish", we have to wait for Virgil, and this would logically suggest the unprofitable question—once so popular in its crudest form—whether Virgil was a "greater poet" than Lucretius. If, by "greater", the ques-tion refers to genius, there is no answer possible, at least for us moderns, who do not care to arrange men of genius in order of merit, although in ancient times an overwhelming majority of votes would have preferred Virgil as far more "national" a poet than Lucretius.[3] If, however, we think of *art*, our answer must be that the art of the Augustans differs widely from that of the Republicans, but is not necessarily for that reason superior. The de-

[1] I have here adopted the view expressed by such critics as George Saintsbury and Middleton Murry. So does S. Alexander in *British Journal of Psychology*, vol. xvii (1926–7), p. 305 f.

[2] Merrill, *Lucretius*, p. 147.

[3] Except in two archaising periods: the first, in the time of Tacitus, the second, during that of Fronto and Gellius, under the Antonines.

cision would of course depend on individual taste, from which, proverbially, there is no appeal. But there is this much to be said: the taste of the present generation has very markedly changed in a form of art cognate to poetry. In sculpture, Praxiteles, and even Pheidias, have been dethroned, and the artists of the pediments at Olympia reign in their stead. In place of the Apollo Belvedere our grandfathers preferred the Elgin marbles; now, it seems, the Parthenon must yield to the "Maidens" of the Acropolis—or to even earlier specimens of Greek art; and we all know that modern sculptors have set—or followed—this fashion (even to negroid extremes) in their own work. Logically, therefore, by this criterion of taste, Lucretius need not fear "comparison" with the Augustans.

Virgil made striking alterations on the Lucretian model, some of which—notably the use of the paragraph, of caesura, elision, and the like—have been generally approved; but in assonance and alliteration, he followed his model, if with a certain reserve. He admired and often imitated the older poet, not least in verbal effects, so that, in one of his most beautiful lines, he could write *ripae ulterioris amore* to match the harmony of Lucretius in such music as

cuncta coloribus egregiis et odoribus opplet.[1]

[1] v. 740.

46

There is no need to go further into these familiar
details, for either poet; but it may be added that
both "hunted the letter", not only for the pure
pleasure of rhyme but because they discovered that
the repetition of sounds gave a real significance to
their expression. At a time when language was
commonly thought to be "natural"—and, as we
shall see, the Epicureans held that words were
originally suggested by Nature—there was every
reason to choose particular collocations of words
because the sense was emphasised or explained by
the sound. For instance, the "v" in *vis, vita, ventus*
was thought to express life, violence, or force;
"m" implied might or magnitude, owing to the
common *magnus*. Hence, no doubt, the effective
alliteration in such Lucretian lines as

> *magnos manibus divellere montes*
> *multaque vivendo vitalia vincere saecla.*[1]

Of course, the key-words of a "natural" language
were numerous; the "m" in *mors, miser* could also
suggest "death" or "misery", and the result is the
splendid line

> *mortalem vitam mors cum immortalis ademit.*[2]

This special significance of alliteration is quite distinct from the normal repetition, which in origin
is simply due to the instinct for some form of
rhyme—a feeling that can hardly be analysed. In

[1] i. 201 f.   [2] iii. 869.

verse, we may be content with the explanation that such "artful aids" help to build the pattern— the rhythm which Aristotle recognised to be at least one of the "causes" of poetry.[1]

The Choice of words was intimately bound up with a cognate enquiry on which Peripatetic critics laid much emphasis—the search for "Beautiful" words. In this connection, we naturally think first of Longinus, whose phrase is unforgettable: "beautiful words are the actual light of the mind".[2] But the idea had a long history, reaching at least to Aristotle (if not the sophists of the fifth century). Theophrastus had defined τὸ καλὸν ὄνομα as a word which gives pleasure to the ear or sight, or has value to the mind—as we should say, beautiful in itself or for associations.[3] That a word may be beautiful to the ear will hardly be disputed; but no doubt we think chiefly of beautiful words in connection with their associations and suggestions. Such words may be either common or rare; as Horace, after Neoptolemus or some other Peripatetic source, well remarked,

> dixeris egregie, notum si callida verbum
> reddiderit iunctura novum,[4]

that is, skilful arrangement will give new signifi-

---

[1] See further *Roman Poetry*, ch. VII, where I elaborated these views with special reference to Lucretius and Catullus.

[2] *De Subl.* 30. 1.

[3] See *Greek View of Poetry*, p. 162.　　　　[4] *Ars Poet.* 47 f.

cance to a well-known word; and Coleridge pointed out that the common becomes uncommon "in those places" where Wordsworth was most successful.

Lucretius is full of these happy alliances of usual words combined to produce an unusual effect. We may think first, perhaps, of the *flammantia moenia mundi*, in which a familiar adjective and an equally familiar substantive unite to express all the majesty in the flaming ramparts of the Universe. Or, again, in the passage (quoted above) which impressed Bentley, there is the noble union of *signa* with *severa*, where certain unpoetic Germans altered the adjective to *serena*, oblivious of *severa silentia* elsewhere in Lucretius, and ignorant of Keats, in his conscious or unconscious echo—the "earnest stars". In the same class is the collocation of two simple substantives, *flammai flos*—suggesting, almost literally, the "flowering of the lonely word"—in a metaphor still fresh for Lucretius, if, later, the flower of fire was to be overworked by Swinburne. Not that all the imaginative effects fall within this Wordsworthian category. Lucretius often makes good use of the rare word. In *Summania templa*, for example, the unusual epithet derived from the little-known god Summanus brings out the grandeur of the sky by night, matching the glory of the sun by day—*radiatum insigne diei*. Nor does the poet altogether disdain a Greek adjective in *daedala tellus*, where the epithet would have pleased Horace

—parce distorta—as it was afterwards to please
Shelley in his "daedal earth".[1] He tries a few
other experiments in Graecism,[2] but there is in the
De Rerum Natura nothing of that riot of Greek
words which the Neoterics affected. His poetry is
more manifest in the simplicity of which examples
have already been quoted—in the *otia dia*, for that
divine ease that is in the hills on earth, as in the
quiet homes of the gods—*per loca pastorum deserta
atque otia dia*. And, finally, there is the solemn
beauty of *mors immortalis*—the phrase that sums up
the whole Epicurean philosophy of death.

One class of unusual words must here be mentioned: the compound adjective. This form played
so large a part in all Greek poetry that it was bound
to be imitated by the early Roman verse-writers,
especially as compounds in general (*ambarvalia,
suovetaurilia*, etc.) were not alien to the genius of
old Latin. Pacuvius, Lucilius and other pioneers
made various experiments, some of which, like *re-
pandirostrum* and *incurvicervicum*, were hardly "beautiful" words, and offended such purists as Persius,
Quintilian and Gellius. Cicero, in his verse, was
more cautious, but his compound adjectives (e.g.
vastificus, multiplicabilis) are dull and fairly obvious.[3]

[1] *Hymn of Pan.*

[2] Notably in dealing with music (ii. 412, 505) and "hypo-
coristic" love-words (iv. 1160 f.).

[3] A list of Ciceronian compounds is given by Ewbank, *op. cit.*
p. 220. On the general subject see *Roman Poetry*, p. 228 f.

Catullus, a real poet, could do far better: when his inspiration was most Hellenic, as in the *Atys*, his epithets—*silvicultrix*, *nemorivagus* and the like—were splendid additions to the Roman poetic vocabulary. Lucretius has many striking compounds, whether Ennian, as *laetificus*, or probably of his own coinage, as *silvifragus*, *fluctifragus*, *caecigenus*, *noctivagus*, *levisomnus*, and many others, to most of which it would be difficult to refuse the title of "beautiful". All these pictorial adjectives, however, were pruned away by the Augustans, who confined themselves to the simplest composites (in *-fer*, *-ger*, *-sonus*, *-modus*, *-potens*, etc.), apparently on the ground that the others offended the genius of Latinity, in spite of Horace's express permission—which he himself rarely took—to use new forms (especially from the Greek) with a modest licence.[1] It is the more remarkable that this Augustan purity was violated by the post-Augustan poets, who frequently revived the compound adjective, after a century of neglect.

From isolated "beautiful" words we may turn to their collocation in the rhythm of the line, or series of lines. The development of hexameter verse, as a thing of beauty, is a subject familiar to all classical students, and need here be touched on very briefly, and only in special connection with Lucretius. In general, it may be said that

[1] *Ars Poet.* 50 f.

the archaism of his rhythm corresponds with the
archaism of his language. Let us first take the
single line by itself. The early experimenters in the
art of translating the Greek hexameter must have
been struck (like Matthew Arnold) by its rapidity.
Homer of course can be spondaic, but he is
primarily dactylic, and there are passages in Ennius
which are as rapid as the first line of the *Odyssey*.[1]
Lucretius, too, is formally much more Homeric
than Virgil, whose main object seems to have been
to slow down the pace of epic, suiting it, both by
elision and spondaic rhythm, to the natural strength
and dignity of the Latin language, which expressed the *gravitas* of the Roman character at its
best. Lucretian hexameters, while normally lighter
and more speedy—as witness the invocation to
Venus and many other carefully written passages—
admit far more variation, in *tempo*, than the *Aeneid*.
The rhythm is still experimental, and has not
settled down. Yet Lucretius has an ear which
responds to a far wider range of sound than the
subtle harmonies which Virgil approved. The
younger poet, of course, often suited his line to the
sense, as in his famous *procumbit humi bos* or *quadrupe-
dante putrem sonitu quatit ungula campum*; but Lucretius goes much further, undeterred by Augustan
classicism. We may take as two examples, out of

[1] Cf. the passage beginning *excita cum tremulis* (fr. *Ann.* i.
xxv *c*).

many, a couple of single lines which illustrate the present point. The first is

et membratim vitalem deperdere sensum,

on which Munro remarked that it "is the most effective instance of sound answering to sense, produced by the simplest means, that I know of in the whole range of Latin poetry". The second is even better known:

prava cubantia prona supina atque absona tecta,[1]

where the faultiness of a building is finely expressed by an hexameter equally faulty according to Augustan "canons". The most striking feature of the Latin hexameter, as perfected by Virgil, is of course the construction of the paragraph with its almost infinite variation of "running-over" and pauses within the line. Homer had rarely aimed at this effect—the Greek hexameter was usually self-contained—and Ennius followed the Greek practice. In this and other respects, Lucretius stands between Ennius and Virgil. His object was to bring Ennius up to date, while holding to the Ennian tradition. That pioneer had scarcely succeeded in creating an homogeneous vehicle of expression. Among the fragments of the *Annals*—they number only about 600 lines or parts of lines—there are indeed whole passages which even now do not jar by reason of

[1] iii. 527; iv. 517.

53

broken, uncorrelated rhythms; but Ennius had not discovered a norm of variety within homogeneity. He has violent oscillations between extremes, as witness the over-spondaic line

olli respondet rex Albai Longai,

and the over-dactylic

at tuba terribili sonitu taratantara dixit.

The verse-pattern is not so much varied as broken.

It remained for Cicero to pare away both these extremes, and so to create a style which should neither limp, like the King of Alba Longa, nor canter, like the sound of the terrible trumpet. Cicero's ear, at least, was seldom at fault, whatever may be the defects of his poetic inspiration. The debt of Lucretius to Cicero's early poems has long been recognised, but it is only in recent years that the reference of Plutarch to the orator as accounted, for a time, the first poet in Rome, has been fully appraised.[1] His use of the hexameter marks a real turning-point in Latin poetry, and deserves the reminder, "it is often forgotten that when Cicero first handled this metre he had little more than the work of Ennius and Lucilius on which to model it".[2] But his rhythms were few and tame, and it was Lucretius who rescued the hexameter from the uncouthness of Ennius and the mannerisms

---

[1] *Life of Cicero*, 2. [2] Ewbank, *op. cit.* p. 3.

of the Neoterics. Of these, Catullus, at least, being a lyrical genius, never acquired the Virgilian freedom of the hexameter. His excursion into the style of the epic—the *Peleus and Thetis*, technically a "little epic" or *epyllion*—is so monotonous in rhythm that its artifice would have been quite intolerable if the poem had been extended to the length of the *De Rerum Natura*. Catullus hunts two mannerisms to death: (i) the spondaic ending, and (ii) varieties of the "Golden" line. The first (of the type *carmine compellabo*) is by no means confined to proper names, where even Virgil admitted the use, but followed the Alexandrians, who so largely developed the old Homeric practice, that the spondee in the fifth foot became a sort of sign-manual for the Neoterics or *Graecissantes*. Cicero's contemptuous allusion to these *cantores Euphorionis*[1] has a particular reference to this mannerism, which is rare in Lucretius; indeed its total absence in the Sixth book has been taken as a proof that the poet's dislike of the νεώτεροι grew during the course of his work. Nor has Lucretius much use for the Golden line, of the type

caerula verrentes abiegnis aequora palmis

(grammatical agreement indicated by a c b a b) which, with variations, played so large a part in Catullus, and was afterwards to be exploited *ad*

[1] *Tusc.* iii. 45.

nauseam by Lucan.[1] Once or twice he strikes a
Catullan note, as in the beautiful passage:

> *insatiabiliter deflevimus, aeternumque*
> *nulla dies nobis maerorem e pectore demet;*

but the norm of Catullus here becomes a rare and
pleasing divagation. Like Cicero, Lucretius seldom
pauses within the compass of a line; but there is an
equivalent for the Virgilian paragraph in the rush
and swirl of his hexameters, which vary in length
between the epigrammatic end-stop of

> *tantum religio potuit suadere malorum*

and a final pause at the close of a sustained period.

The Alexandrians were nearest the Romans not
only in time but in type of civilisation, and it is
not surprising that no Latin poet was entirely free
from their influence. What *is* surprising is that, at
a time when the Latin Neoterics were in full possession of the field, Lucretius should have been the
only poet to resist their innovations. His models
were taken from the older Greeks—not only Empedocles but Homer, Sappho, Aeschylus, Euripides,
Thucydides—just as he harked back to the older
Roman heroes, Ancus and the Scipios, for his
"examples".

In art, then, as well as in genius, it may be
claimed that Lucretius amply justified the favour-

[1] Strictly, the "Golden" line starts with two adjectives followed
by a verb, and two substantives at the end. Lines such as i. 9:
placatumque nitet diffuso lumine caelum (a c b b a), are rare in Lucretius.

able criticism of Cicero. We may go further, and
agree with those who have placed the poet in
the highest category—the class of Homer and
Sophocles, of Virgil, of Dante, Shakespeare and
Milton. He fulfils all the canons of ὑψότης—eleva-
tion—laid down by Longinus, even if that critic
advisedly refrained from trespassing on the ground
of Roman poets. Everyone knows Arnold's para-
phrase of the Longinian hall-marks: the grand
style arises in poetry, when a noble nature, poetically gifted, treats with simplicity, or with severity,
a serious subject—a definition which has been
slightly emended: "a great subject made great by
the greatness of the poet's mind".[1] We may, if
we will, apply to Lucretius the admission that
Homer's rare slips gave Longinus "no pleasure".
The Roman poet, however, has the quality of his
defects. That quality arises from the enthusiasm
stimulating a teacher who urges his pupil to study,
even with disagreement, every detail in his creed:

si tibi vera videntur,
dede manus, aut si falsum est, accingere contra.

And these details, even if "true", are not en-
couraging to the lover of pure poetry. But there
is a full compensation for the minutiae of Atomism
in the *furor arduus* of the "learned" Lucretius,
whose learning, as I have tried to show, was
tempered by the equal aid of Genius and Art.

[1] J. Bailey in *Essays and Studies* (English Association), vol. ii.

CHAPTER III

EPICURUS

Epicurus was born at Samos in 342 or 341 B.C.
He was technically an Athenian citizen, his father,
Neocles, being a colonist from the Attic *deme* of
Gargettus, who taught as a schoolmaster on the
island. Various stories were current about his boyhood, one of which is plausible enough, although
it may be due to a desire to prove that the child
was father of the man: it was said that he was
reading the *Theogony*, and found that his teacher
could not explain the beginning of things; according to Hesiod, all came from Chaos, but the
enquiring boy asked: How did Chaos arise? As a
young man (in 323 B.C.) he went to Athens to
claim his citizenship and probably to pass the
regular period of military service as an *ephebus*. In
the following year the colonists were expelled from
Samos, and Neocles fled to Colophon, where he
was joined by Epicurus. The next date of which
we can be certain is 310 B.C., when we hear that
he taught philosophy in Mitylene, and about 306
B.C. he returned to Athens, where he settled—
apart from visits to Asia Minor—until his death
in 270 B.C. At Athens, the famous Garden became
the centre of a school in which the Master lived

in close association with his pupils—male and female; indeed the Epicureans, both then and afterwards, laid so much stress on the value of friendship that the sect has not improperly been called an ancient Society of Friends. Epicureanism was both a communion and a way of life, not least adapted to the average man or woman, who lacked the ability or inclination to study more difficult philosophies. It has often been pointed out that this Society, with its indifference to sex and social or national status, has an analogue in the early Christian Church.[1]

To some extent, the cultivation of such friendship had in post-Alexandrian times taken the place which had been occupied by politics in the old city-state. From the earliest period, it is true, the Greeks had always cultivated and idealised personal friendship, as shown in the typical examples of Achilles and Patroclus, Theseus and Pirithous, Orestes and Pylades; but, so far, only the schools of Pythagoras and Plato had anticipated the close ties of familiar association that bound the Epicurean society. The Founder himself, to judge from his letters and other fragments, as well as from outside testimony, was eminently a man to inspire friendship. Whilst holding that its genesis was purely selfish, from the need of help,

[1] See A. E. Taylor, *Epicurus*, pp. 28 and 92; W. Wallace, *Epicureanism*, p. 63.

Epicurus insisted on its supreme value, and rose
to almost lyrical heights—an attitude rare to
his temperament—in affirming that "friendship
dances round the world proclaiming to us all to
awake and praise the happy life".[1] And again,
"Of all the things that wisdom acquires for the
happiness of the whole life, far the greatest is the
possession of friendship". The wise man should
indeed aim at self-sufficiency (αὐτάρκεια), but
Epicurus is less concerned with this ideal than the
Stoics, and seems to have regarded friendship as
the equivalent for the individual of the Social
Contract for the tribe. There was to be a "compact of the wise",[2] and, when Lucretius dedicated
his poem to Memmius, in the hope of his "plea-
surable friendship", the words almost certainly
convey an invitation to join the Brotherhood.[3]

This Brotherhood started as a society for mutual
protection (ἀσφάλεια), and its original members
were taught to be under no illusion of altruism.
For very practical reasons, Epicurus held that
friendship was a "necessary" pleasure[4]—it struck
the mean between indifference or dislike, and
sexual passion, which often involved pain, and
was therefore unnecessary and a "pleasure" to be

[1] Fr. v. 52 Bailey. Hartel's φιλοσοφία for φιλία is unlikely.
[2] *foedus quoddam sapientium* (συνθήκη), Cic. *Fin.* i. 70.
[3] C. Pascal, *Stud.* 6.
[4] See below, p. 95.

60

avoided. At the same time, mere selfishness failed to satisfy natural instincts; and although the school prided themselves on observing their Master's teaching to the letter,[1] it is not surprising that Cicero notes a development, not mentioned by Epicurus, that friendship started with utility, but passed into altruism.[2] The chief thing, no doubt, was a common bond of "security"; it was essential that all members should have the freedom from fear (both of gods and men) in order to enjoy the pure pleasure of collective friendship—and this was probably enough for Epicurus, at least in theory. But his followers, by an easy transition, attached weight to the more personal element—*etiam omissa spe voluptatis*.

The Founder seems to have deserved, by reason of his personality, no less than his philosophy, the admiration of his school, including Lucretius, long after the first settlement of the Garden had been extended to the Roman world. No great teacher, perhaps, has ever suffered more from traducers; but the attacks on Epicurus were plainly inspired by *odium philosophicum*, if not *theologicum*. Even his ancient enemies, Cicero and Seneca,[3] acknowledged that his private life was blameless, although the Brotherhood (which included a Sisterhood) was a cause of scandal. His own sect had nothing

[1] Diog. L. x. 9.   [2] Cic. *Fin*. ii. 82.
[3] Cic. *Fin*. ii. 81; Seneca, *De Vita Beata*, 13.

61

but praise for their Master's character. Diogenes
Laertius, writing what may be called an official
Life of Epicurus, gives the direct lie to his calum-
niators, and describes his "benevolence to all"—
his devotion to parents, his generosity to brothers
and his gentleness to slaves. Diogenes also remarks on the fact that his school continued to exist
after almost all the others had come to an end.[1]
His biographer goes on to eulogise him for reverence to the gods and asceticism—two characteristics which later critics unfairly denied.

Fragments of his private letters go far to bear
out this favourable estimate of Epicurus. In particular, there is a delightful letter written to a
child, bidding him (or her) to be "always obedient
to papa and Matro...I and all the rest of us love
you sincerely, just because you are always obedient
to them".[2] There is hardly a question of "security",
by the way, to be derived from this friendship with
a child. His correspondence must have shown
more vigour than appears in his "esoteric" work,
the only certain specimen of which is the letter to
a pupil called Herodotus—a dull and not very
lucid epitome of his physics and general principles.
The letter to Menoeceus (iii), composed in a more

---

[1] Diog. L. x. 9. The date of Diogenes is placed early in the
third century. See Sandys, *Hist. Class. Schol.* vol. i, p. 332. On
the later history of the school see below.

[2] Bailey, fr. 35.

familiar, "exoteric" style, is much brighter and more readable; that written to Pythocles (ii) covers the ground of the Sixth book of Lucretius, but its authenticity has been doubted since early classical times, although it entirely agrees with the teaching of Epicurus.

So far, we have an attractive picture of a man capable of both feeling and inspiring affection, but not necessarily a great man. There are, in fact, certain blots in the character of Epicurus which his ancient critics noticed. He seems to have claimed "originality", beyond even the limits allowed in antiquity, and not only denied his dependence on previous philosophers, but had the bad taste to laugh at them. Heraclitus, "the obscure", may have been fair game; but he ridiculed his own model, Democritus, by a poor joke (Ληρόκριτος) and said disrespectful things about Nausiphanes, a later atomist to whom he must also have been in debt.[1] Here Lucretius, who quotes "the revered opinion of great Democritus", even when he disapproves of it, shows more decency,[2] although it is only right to say that elsewhere Epicurus seems to have treated Democritus with respect.

A few words should here be added on the subject of his health, since it has often been argued that his bodily weakness (which is well attested) was to

[1] Cic. *Fin.* i. 21; Diog. L. x. 8. [2] iii. 371.

some extent responsible for certain features in his outlook on life. A subdued theory of pleasure, an advice to abstain from politics, a general quiescence,[1] a self-restraint in food and drink—all these seemed to be a reflection of his ill-health, which enemies were not slow to exploit, and probably to exaggerate. But there is really nothing in Epicureanism that can certainly be attributed to a valetudinarian. If "weakness" comes into the reckoning at all, we should bear in mind the unhealthiness, not of an individual, but of Greece under tyrants, and of Rome in the late Republic. Epicurus himself showed a fortitude, true to his philosophy, during the last years of his life, when he suffered a painful and fatal illness.

The charm of his personality is shown not only by the devotion of his friends, but by a fine bust (in the Capitoline Museum)[2] which expresses a dignity and firmness of character, not unworthy of an ascetic who was also, in some respects, a man of the world; at the same time the head, with its overarching brows, heavy nose and clear-cut mouth, goes far to explain a certain lack of humour—Epicurus was no Plato—and also the uncompromising self-assurance of one who insisted, both in

[1] Summed up in the famous advice λάθε βιώσας, "let your life be unseen".

[2] Figured as frontispiece in Bailey's *Epicurus*. For another portrait, in the British Museum, see R. P. Hinks, *Greek and Roman Portraits-Sculpture* (1935), p. 10.

practice and precept, that the wise man should be dogmatic[1]—advice followed by all his school, not least by Lucretius.

A modern philosopher calls Epicurus a saint: "he has at least as much right to the title as some who have been canonised".[2] His Roman followers raised him to the rank of a god,[3] and Lucretius more than once expresses in enthusiastic terms his veneration for the Master, who as Saviour of mankind deserved divinity.[4] In his praises of Epicurus, one passage, in the Third book, may stand for all, though the Introduction to the Fifth book is even more eulogistic, with its definite claim that his teacher should be ranked among the gods rather than Ceres or Liber or Hercules:

Thee, who didst lift on high a beacon-light,
Afire in the dark, and first illuminate
The happy life, thee, glory of the Greeks,
I follow, and in thy foot-prints plant mine own,
Fain, not so much to rival, as for love
To imitate thee. How should swallow vie

[1] Diog. L. x. 121 b. Cf. Cic. *Fin.* ii. 21; *sane fidenter*, *N.D.* i. 18.
[2] G. Santayana in *Three Philosophical Poets*.
[3] Cic. *Tusc.* i. 48.
[4] Lucr. i. 62 f., iii. 1–13, 1042 f., v. 1–54, vi. 1–34. The repeated Introductions suggest that Lucretius "began with Epicurus" in imitation of old hymns which "began with Zeus". Each Introduction treats of Epicurus in a different aspect, sometimes suggested by the subject of the particular book: in i, the eulogy is for the destroyer of popular religion; in iii, for the discoverer of Nature; in v and vi, for the ethical teacher.

With swan? How may the kid, with tremulous limbs,
Challenge the fiery steed to equal race?
To thee, our father, Nature stands revealed—
Our father and our teacher; from thy pages,
As bees that taste each blossom in flowery glen,
We rifle all the golden treasure of words—
The golden words worth everlasting life.

iii, 1–13.

The title *deus* may surprise those who remember
that the Epicurean gods were kings without
thrones, playing no part in human affairs. In one
sense, of course, it was a mere compliment, better
given to Epicurus than to Demetrius Poliorcetes,
deified by the servile Athenians about the very
year in which the philosopher came to the city.
In another sense, the title was a counterblast to the
Stoics; their patron Heracles—as Lucretius protested—did less for mankind than one who had
freed men from terror of the gods. And finally
the honour was due to a genuine appreciation of
the only teacher, between Pythagoras and Chris-
tianity, whose personality was strong enough to
impress his name upon his school. They may have
argued that Empedocles was a god, in his own
estimation; why should not Epicurus, who had
done far more for mankind, be divine? Moreover,
his personal life was a splendid example of that
"calm" (ἀταραξία) which belonged to the perfect
happiness of the Epicurean gods. To such a degree
of divinity any of his followers might (at least in

theory) attain, as Epicurus himself allows;[1] Lucretius boasts that reason can so far prevail over the defects of human nature

ut nil impediat dignam dis degere vitam.[2]

For some time past, a search for the "perfect" man, who should be the (philosophic) Saviour, had been in the air, no doubt owing to the inspiring personality of Socrates. But even the Stoics hardly claimed Socrates as a flawless example of perfection. He was too human to represent a school which prided itself on denying some of the most natural instincts of humanity. They made shift by putting their paragon into commission, distributing his virtues among the heroes of mythology—Heracles and Odysseus, as well as Socrates. The Epicureans were more fortunate in that they needed to go no farther than their founder, whose influence, both during and after his life, was, as we have seen, the strongest asset of the school.

As may be expected, however, there have been many to dispute the claim of his followers that he was a great teacher as well as an inspiring personality. In particular, he has been denied originality. He boasted of being self-taught, whereas his opponents—Cicero and others—accused him

---

[1] Ep. iii. *ad fin.*: ζήσεις δὲ ὡς θεὸς ἐν ἀνθρώποις.
[2] iii. 320–323.

of hardly changing the ideas of Democritus, the one important variation (the atomic swerve) being, in their view, ridiculous. As his physical system was merely preliminary to his ethics, in which his teaching could scarcely be thought unoriginal, his debt to earlier atomists would not much detract from his greatness. But some modern scholars have agreed with his ancient enemies, holding that, while the personal influence of Epicurus was immense, his mind was unfitted for abstruse speculation.[1] On the other hand, it has been argued that he was logical (though he despised formal logic) and was a great systematiser, comparable with such thinkers as Bentham and Herbert Spencer.[2] This is a fairer estimate than that of Ciceronian or patristic invective.[3] But the latest student of Epicurus goes much further in rehabilitating the Master's achievement: his originality is not only apparent in the kinetics of Atomism, but in the history of anthropology (including the growth of language), and even in psychology. In all these departments, Dr Bailey sees evidence for the "workings of a great mind".[4] More than this, the

[1] E.g. W. Wallace, *op. cit.* p. 239.

[2] R. D. Hicks, *Stoic and Epicurean*, p. 198.

[3] For a very unfavourable estimate of Epicureanism as "a clumsy amalgam of inconsistent beliefs", and other hard sayings, see A. E. Taylor, *op. cit.* p. 25, etc.

[4] C. Bailey, *Greek Atomists*; where see especially pp. 299, 437, 481, 528, 533.

Epicurean religion—in my opinion—marks a distinct step in advance of the crude Hellenic thought; and, finally, the peculiar turn which Epicurus gave to the doctrine of Pleasure, radically different from all previous conceptions of the *summum bonum*, stamps him not only as an earnest moralist but as a highly independent thinker.

None the less, whatever his originality, Epicurus was a thorough Greek, following the spirit of the Delphic advice, μηδὲν ἄγαν, "nothing too much". His *aurea dicta* might often be called the message of *aurea mediocritas*. In many respects, he mediated and compromised between the various extremes of opinion, to which Greek thinkers were prone. His theology held the balance between the agnosticism of Protagoras and the accepted Olympian religion. His humanism was the Mean of two opposite views about mankind—that of Plato, and that of the Cynics. He could not accept Platonic idealism; but, on the other hand, he revolted from the Cynical Return to Nature, which too often meant, not human, but bestial nature. In ethics, again, he stood midway: rejecting the frank sensuality of Aristippus, he equally rejected the Stoic paradoxes and pratings about Virtue.

The system of Epicurus will be chiefly discussed in connection with Lucretius, but meanwhile it may be convenient to summarise his position. Of the preceding philosophies two, at least—the Pla-

tonic and Aristotelian—were so elaborate, and
perhaps so difficult, as to have no message for the
less intelligent or less educated Greek. In the days
of Socrates and the sophists average Athenians
may have had some interest in speculation—
Socrates freely questioned the carpenter and the
shoemaker, even if their answers were not always
satisfactory; and, as we learn from the *Clouds*,
Aristophanes had turned the great philosopher
into a laughing-stock for all Athens on the comic
stage. But, in the main, philosophy had been confined to the aristocrats—whether these were aristocratic by birth or by intelligence. No doubt the
Epicurean philosophy was itself, in one sense, not
"easy"; the details of the atomic theory are difficult enough, as any modern attempt to unravel
their complications will amply show. But Epicurus,
who had not been in touch with elementary school-
teaching for nothing, constructed his ethical system
for anyone to understand, not least for the ordinary
simple-minded man and woman. His voluminous
works were of various classes: esoteric, addressed
to the more initiated follower; exoteric, to those
who had not altogether "arrived"; and, finally,
there was a kind of Catechism, or Articles (forty
in number), written in short and pithy sentences,
by which the veriest beginner could grasp the
essentials of the creed. Of these Articles, the first
four were later known collectively as the Quadruple

Remedy (against ignorance),[1] summing up the chief points of the system, as a creed which both taught the real nature of the gods and mortality, and laid down the principles of a moral life, with the definition of Pleasure as the End.

By such means the appeal of philosophy was extended to reach the large majority of citizens in Athens and elsewhere, for whom no great interest in the finer points of metaphysics had ever existed. People needed a practical, workaday system—a way of life, a re-orientation of the old ethical view in its relation to the autonomous city-state. In the past the democrats had been more or less fully occupied in the government of their city. Now, with the Macedonian conquest, there was no free city left to govern itself. Ethics had ceased to be a branch of Politics; even in the time of Aristotle, the connection had been an anachronism, which Aristotle himself had not the perspective to notice. The loss of independence resulted in a rapid disappearance of the old social theory of ethics. Even in the beginning of the fourth century the political aspect of morality had been undermined by such individualists as Antisthenes, Diogenes and Aristippus; but these "citizens of the world" were, after all, only voices in opposition. A catastrophe was needed to change the views of a minority into an

---

[1] τετραφάρμακος. See Epicur. *Ep.* iii. 123 f. These articles are quoted in this book under the abbreviation Κ.Δ. (κύριαι δόξαι).

accepted outlook. The battle of Chaeronea (338 B.C.) is a real landmark for this change to a philosophy, at once cosmopolitan (as the Greeks understood the word) and individualistic, although there are some who doubt whether this battle, just preceding Aristotle's death (332 B.C.), can be taken as giving a definite date of the transition. It has sometimes been urged that there was no real break in the historical continuity, and that at least the seeds of post-Aristotelian ethics were much older.[1] But, as I have argued, there is a great difference between the seed and its development into fruit. Epicurus is the fruit, of which Democritus had been the seed. The metaphor is perhaps inexact, since it applies only to one part of Epicureanism, and that part the least important in the Founder's opinion. He was forced to start with physics, but a study of external nature was a mere preliminary to ethics, the proper study of Hellenistic man. In order to understand the Atomism which Epicurus adopted, it is necessary to go back even beyond his immediate "originals".

ATOMISM

A very brief reference to pre-Democritean philosophy may be sufficient to account for Atomism itself. Starting from the premiss that all things are essentially One, earlier thinkers had been faced

[1] See A. E. Taylor, *op. cit.* p. 2 f.

with the problem of reconciling the apparent
change and flux of phenomena with this monism.
Parmenides denied that motion existed—the One
could not be Many; our senses were at fault.
Heraclitus had already held that "eyes and ears
are bad witnesses", and the immediate issue was
to decide between those who upheld the value of
the senses, and those who discredited or denied
sense-perception. The negativism of Parmenides
led to a question which has since become the first
problem of philosophy. If phenomena are illusive,
the illusion no less exists, and must somehow be
explained. The problem was therefore not concerned to answer the question: *What* is there to
know? but *How* are we to know it, whatever it
may be? Are we to trust our senses or our reason?
If sense-perception and reason contradict each
other, which of the two is to be trusted? All schools
after Parmenides had therefore to start with the
basis of knowledge, and it became necessary to
re-examine the value of the senses, as well as to
criticise the Parmenidean conception of (material)
monism. Empedocles and Anaxagoras were mainly
concerned with the task of correcting the monism
which implied that the Universe was a *plenum*
($\pi\lambda\tilde{\eta}\rho\epsilon\varsigma$), and that the apparent motion of phenomena had no real existence. In order to introduce
change and motion, it was imperative to assume
a *number* of existing things, and this step was taken

by Empedocles and—in a different way—by Anaxagoras. The systems of these two were criticised
by the Epicureans.[1] Here, it need only be remarked that neither philosopher—Empedocles with
his four elements, or Anaxagoras with his Oppo-
sites and Seeds—went far enough. As Burnet says,
"a pluralism which stops short of atomism will
achieve no permanent result".

The important step was taken by Leucippus[2]
and the more celebrated Democritus, Plato's contemporary. Their basic principles were that (i)
nothing is created out of nothing; (ii) nothing is
destroyed into nothing; (iii) nothing happens by
chance, but everything is by a cause and necessity;[3] (iv) nothing exists but atoms and void (empty
space). Void can neither touch nor be touched,
and is the only incorporeal thing allowed by the
atomists to have an independent existence. The
distinctive principle is the introduction of this void
or space, whose existence is also shown by Lucretius
to be as much self-evident as that of body.[4] The
formation of the Universe is due to an endless fall
of atoms through infinite void, in which Democritus held that greater (and therefore heavier)
atoms fell more quickly, so that worlds continually

[1] See Lucr. i.

[2] J. Burnet, *Early Greek Philosophy*, ed. 2, ch. ix.

[3] Necessity (ἀνάγκη) is a general conception of Natural Law;
see Bailey, *op. cit.* p. 120 f.

[4] i. 329–448, 483–527.

74

arise by their collision. Aristotle, however, pointed out that in a vacuum all bodies must fall with equal velocity,[1] and therefore no such collisions could occur. This objection led Epicurus to a very practical development: he substituted a swerve of atoms (παρέγκλισις, in Lucretius, *clinamen*) which should cause collision laterally, instead of vertically. Atoms, Lucretius said, must move through void *incerto tempore incertisque locis*—"otherwise Nature would never have created anything".[2]

The swerve must be the least possible (*nec plus quam minimum*), because the senses prove that oblique motion in such conditions is impossible; but, as the human eye cannot see whether bodies fall in an *absolutely* straight line, a slight swerve is not incompatible with the evidence of the senses, on which Lucretius here, as elsewhere, relies;[3] it being a flaw in the Epicurean system that evidence was admitted not only positively, as derived from the senses, but negatively, as not definitely contradicted by them, provided of course that the argument required this admission.[4]

The theory of atomic swerve seemed ridiculous—or worse—to those ancient critics who believed in

[1] *Fragm. Phys.* 2 Mullach, p. 358. See F. A. Lange, *Hist. of Materialism*, ed. 3 (1925), vol. i, p. 26.

[2] ii. 216–293.

[3] The passage is discussed by Masson, vol. i, ch. x. For the general theory see Giussani, vol. i, pp. 97–124.

[4] See further ch. ix.

Providence, such as Cicero and Plutarch. "If", it was asked, "there is no First Cause to move the atoms, how did this deflection arise?"[1] Modern critics have pointed out that Epicurus here showed a flagrant contempt for the laws of cause and effect, since he assigned no cause for the swerve. Of course, the deviation had to be assumed for two reasons, both essential to Epicurus, and at the very root of his physics and ethics alike—not only did it account for the existence of a self-moved universe, including innumerable worlds besides our own (since atoms were infinite in number), but it led to the doctrine of Spontaneity or Free-will in Man, which he required as the basis of his ethics. Otherwise, how could men choose between the pure and the impure pleasures? How, indeed, could men and *a fortiori* animals fail to be mere automata? At best, a denial of *voluntas* would lead to the Stoic "acquiescence" in destiny—*ducunt volentem fata, nolentem trahunt*;[2] at worst, it would mean complete fatalism, in which the absence of choice precludes all moral responsibility.

The adoption of the swerve was therefore quite deliberate. No doubt, as Bailey says, it is a fault in Epicureanism, "from the point of view of ultimate consistency, but it is not to be treated as a petty expedient to get over a temporary difficulty,

---

[1] Cic. *N.D.* i. 25. 69; *De Fat.* 10. 22; *Fin.* i. 19; Plut. *De Soll. Anim.* 7, p. 964 E.   [2] Seneca, *Ep.* 107. 11.

or an unintelligent mistake which betrays the super-
ficial thinker".[1] Indeed, both Masson[2] and Bailey
remark that some such swerve is contemplated by
all neo-materialists, to account for consciousness,
if that is ultimately to be derived from inorganic
matter, whether called "world-stuff", "psycho-
plasm", or something which, like the fourth essence of the Lucretian mind-atom, is nameless.[3]

From an ethical point of view, the question of
Free-will is, of course, all-important; and it is not
surprising that Epicurus found the theory of Atomic
Swerve as useful in his morals as in his physics.
In the words of Lucretius, spontaneity, "wrested
from the fates", is a power common to all creatures
—*animantibus*:

> *libera per terras unde haec animantibus exstat,*
> *unde est haec, inquam, fatis avolsa voluntas*
> *per quam progredimur quo ducit quemque voluptas?*[4]

In the case of animals, perhaps, this *libera voluntas*
may be better called "spontaneous initiative",
but is scarcely to be dignified by the name of free-
will. The question remains whether man has free-
will, and here the passages in Lucretius and
Epicurus himself are decisive. In the letter to

---

[1] *Op. cit.* p. 321.
[2] Masson, *op. cit.* ch. x.   [3] See below, p. 104 f.
[4] ii. 256. Cf. iii. 294 f. Animals have *mens* (ii. 260, iii. 295,
299), but this need not include *ratio*. See Cic. *N.D.* i. 48. Only
plants are not ἐμψυχα, Aet. v. 26. 3.

Menoeceus[1] it is definitely stated that some things are within our control, as opposed to other things which happen either by necessity or chance. Wallace[2] is therefore over-cautious in remarking: "it is, perhaps, hazardous in the scanty supply of evidence to attempt a categorical answer to the question" (Has man, according to Epicurus, a free-will?). The letter to Menoeceus, supported by Lucretius, is surely evidence enough, although we may agree with Wallace that the free-will controversy had scarcely formulated itself in the time of Epicurus. But it is clear that, as against the Stoics, who were strict determinists, the Epicureans stood for a degree of human spontaneity which makes them early champions of free-will. In view of the fact that this conception of Nature was entirely fatalistic, the *libera voluntas* has often been thought inconsistent, as modern determinists have pointed out. But since some men of scientific eminence have left open a place for the possibility of a free mind,[3] there is every excuse for Epicurus to have separated human from external Nature. In his logic, he seems to be consistent: the mind is atomic, and its atoms, themselves senseless, have at most the inherent potentiality of spontaneous action. But, taken together, the mind-atoms have

[1] Epicur. *Ep.* iii. 133.　　[2] p. 118.
[3] Sir James Jeans, *New Background of Science*[2], p. 283 f.; Sir Arthur Eddington, *New Pathways in Science*.

the power to choose between several actions. Masson's statement that "free-will exists in the atoms" is misleading, and requires his own correction "in the soul-atoms it is active, and can originate motion, but in the atoms composing dead matter, it is potential only, and can never be 'a cause of motion'".[1] As Bailey explains more succinctly, "the cause of free-will is the conscious aggregate of the ψυχή". Any compound (*concilium*) "has an individuality of its own in which it may acquire qualities and even powers which are not possessed by the individual component atoms".[2]

[1] Masson, vol. ii, p. 129 f.
[2] Bailey on Epicur. *Ep.* iii. 133. 6. See his *Greek Atomists*, p. 435 f.

CHAPTER IV

LIFE OF LUCRETIUS

Lucretius says practically nothing direct about himself, and what others tell us about his life adds little. We do not even know the precise dates of his birth and death. Our authorities—a short passage in Jerome's Eusebian Chronicle, a sentence in Donatus' *Life of Virgil*, a note in a tenth-century manuscript, and the discredited Borgian Life of Lucretius—do not agree. But he was certainly born between 100 and 94 B.C., and died about 55 or 54 B.C. He was undoubtedly a Roman citizen by birth, but it by no means follows that he was born in Rome. That, however, he was at least familiar with the capital is obvious enough from his poem, with its frequent allusions to city life.[1]

His status in Roman society is equally uncertain. The *gens Lucretia* was of course a famous aristocratic clan, if some of its families were plebeian, and it is most likely that the poet was a patrician, although he might conceivably have been a knight. At any rate, the suggestion that he was the son of a freedman, or even an emancipated slave,[2] is extremely improbable, since his tone towards Memmius, a

[1] See Merrill's ed. p. 14.   [2] Marx, *N. Jahr.* (1899), p. 539.

senator and governor of Bithynia, seems to be that
of an equal, not that of the low-born Horace to
Maecenas. The hope to make Memmius a friend
(even if this friendship is not so much personal as
philosophical, by association with the Society of
Friends) could hardly have been felt or expressed
by a mere client; and all the other references to
the nobles show that Lucretius, if he despised the
Roman aristocracy, belonged to that circle. Nor
is there any other improbability that he was nobly
born. In the last century of the Republic, a
number of patricians and knights were to be found
among the Epicureans: Cassius (one of the con-
spirators against Caesar), Atticus, Piso (attacked
by Cicero), Pansa (Caesar's general); and Caesar
himself must have been at least in sympathy with
the school, since, when Pontifex Maximus, he
publicly denied the immortality of the soul.

Indeed, the vogue of Epicureanism, at least in
the first half of the century, so far from being surprising, was inevitable. Most periods of stress and
violence have been accompanied or followed by
intellectual unrest, reflecting the disquiet of political
events. In such crises there must always be many
to agree with the Pauline definition of Epicurean
psychology—Let us eat and drink, for to-morrow
we die. Lucretius, indeed, would have been far
from accepting this psychology as true for himself
or his orthodox friends; but it is none the less

certain that their basic doctrines—both the theory of Pleasure and the denial of Providence—found an easy acceptance in the Rome of Marius and Sulla. During the boyhood of Lucretius, Rome was still engaged in the great turning-point of Italian history—the Social War. Cicero, describing the lawlessness and unhappiness of the city in this age, could mention only a short period of two or three years (85–83 B.C.) when the practice of oratory could be safely resumed.[1] Worse was to come— senators slaughtered in the Forum, and their heads displayed on the Rostra; Rome seized by Sulla, when the battle at the Colline Gate (82 B.C.) was attended by a ghastly massacre of several thousand Samnites, whose cries disturbed the Senate in the temple of Bellona. The wholesale proscriptions by the victor completed his reign of terror; and, long afterwards, Cicero could fear a repetition of this *Sullanum regnum*. In 73 B.C. Lucretius lived through the gladiatorial war of Spartacus, ended by the crucifixion of six thousand prisoners on the Appian Way. He saw, too, the Catilinarian conspiracy, and the troubles leading to the First Triumvirate. While certain politicians—like Cicero himself— could avoid the lure of Epicurus, it is still not wonderful that a poet, with the earnestness and

---

[1] *Brutus*, 90, 308. See generally H. Last in *Cambridge Ancient History*, vol. ix, p. 261; O. Regenbogen, *Lucrez* (Leipzig, 1932), pp. 3 f.

sympathetic inspiration of Lucretius, should have
risen in protest against the horrors of civil war.

Of his life we know nothing whatever, unless we
accept Jerome's statement that Lucretius was maddened by a love-potion, and committed suicide, after
writing his books (which were later "emended"
by Cicero) in the intervals of madness. The story
is perhaps derived from Suetonius, fragments of
whose work *De Viris Illustribus* are extant; but
Suetonius was an inveterate scandal-monger, and
parts, at least, of his tale may be either untrue or
exaggerated. In fact, every one of the details in
this short sentence has been questioned or denied.
The love-potion suggested the subject of Tennyson's fine poem, but has no great intrinsic proba-
bility, although the emperor Gaius was commonly
reported to have been maddened through a love-
philtre administered by his wife Caesonia;[1] and
the suicide is doubtful, if only because Donatus,
as well as Cicero, Nepos and the Augustans are
here silent, and Jerome is not supported by either
Arnobius or Lactantius, who have frequent occasion to mention the work of Lucretius, and who
might be expected to draw a pious conclusion from
the fate of an "atheist".[2] This, no doubt, is only
an *argumentum ex silentio*; but few such arguments
are more vocal. Of course, if Suetonius was the

[1] Suet. *Caligula*, 50; Juv. vi. 610.
[2] See Merrill, p. 16.

authority for the love-potion and consequent suicide, the theory of divine punishment was not
Christian but pagan; there are, however, plenty
of classical tales depending on righteous retribu-
tion—the reputed fate of Euripides and Lucian
(both torn to death by dogs for their impiety) is
in point. It has been thought that the story of
Lucretius' suicide was invented in the Augustan
age, when the emperor tried to restore the Roman
religion;[1] but Virgil's well-known reference to his
predecessor, in the second Georgic—*felix qui potuit
rerum cognoscere causas*—hardly suggests a knowledge of such a tragedy. At any rate, the story—
as Sellar held—"has the air of being the invention
of a late era, to which the name of Lucretius was
probably known merely by a vague reputation".[2]
Reviewing the whole subject, we may not be over-
cautious in doubting, if not dismissing, Jerome's
evidence as "not proven", although some high
authorities have taken one side or the other with
more or less confidence.

The tradition of the poet's insanity is of course
credible, but its truth has been suspected by those
who lay stress on the ambiguity of the word *furor*,
applied by Statius to Lucretius, no doubt in the

[1] G. Giri, *Il Suicidio di Lucrezio* (Palermo, 1895), p. 16 f.
E. Stampini published at Messina an answer to Giri, under the
same title, defending all details of Jerome's "facts".

[2] *Roman Poets of the Republic*, pp. 200–205.

sense of poetic inspiration. Both Christians and
pagans believed Epicureanism to be "mad"—
Horace speaks of the *insaniens sapientia* of his youth,
and the line between genius and madness is proverbially difficult to draw. Believers in the tradition for Lucretius quote (to take English examples
alone) Blake, Cowper, Chatterton, John Clare as
poets writing *per intervalla insaniae*; and readers of
Lombroso could match these names with a still
more formidable list of prose-writers. There is, in
fact, no improbability in the statement, whether
(as various scholars have held) the poet was an
epileptic or otherwise intermittently "mad". His
poem, however, seems to bear no traces of madness; Quintilian complained of its difficulty; but
that great rhetorician was no profound philosopher, and dismissed Lucretius in a brief sentence.
His difficulty is not due to a lack of reasoning
power, even if the poet may not have always fully
understood his authorities. In any case, Lucretius
himself apologised for "obscurity".[1] Cicero had
found it a hard task to invent Latin equivalents
for Greek philosophic terms; his own language
being at the time too concrete for the easy expression of abstract thought. Largely owing to

[1]   *nec me animi fallit Graiorum obscura reperta*
      difficile illustrare Latinis versibus esse,
      multa novis verbis praesertim cum sit agendum
      propter egestatem linguae et rerum novitatem. i. 136 f.

85

Cicero himself the difficulty was overcome, so that medieval philosophy could move with ease in a Latin dress. There was no insuperable defect in the "poverty of the language". But Lucretius did not live to read Cicero's philosophical writings, and he suffered from the additional handicap of metre, in which terms of philosophy were often impossible. With another kind of obscurity—in thought or expression—he had no patience, rebuking Heraclitus, who was here notorious; and his own boast is thoroughly justified:

> quod obscura de re tam lucida pango
> carmina.[1]

The poem itself is so "objective"—so epic in style—that we can learn little about the writer, as distinguished from the poet and philosopher. To all intents and purposes, the author of the *De Rerum Natura* might be anonymous. Unlike Catullus, whose loves and hates are all too apparent; unlike Horace, who could be autobiographical enough in his lyrics as well as his epistles, Lucretius almost wholly sinks the man in his message. His sole lines of personal revelation

> nam neque nos agere hoc patriai tempore iniquo
> possumus aequo animo...[2]

are not *distinctively* a matter of personal experience at all, since they might have been written by any

[1] i. 933.   [2] i. 41.

Epicurean at any time during the civil disturbances. Otherwise we might quote against him (in another connection) his own words

nam verae voces tum demum pectore ab imo
eliciuntur et eripitur persona, manet res,[1]

the mask never drops, to disclose the reality of his private life.

Yet, perhaps, this reticence is not to be regretted. In fact, it is an almost established rule of criticism to hold that, for a poet, only his poetic personality can count, while his life as that of a social or political animal may be neglected.[2] The ancients, when they wrote "Lives" of Homer and Virgil, were too often led by a very human curiosity to insist on unessential details of biography; and Coleridge (in spite of Dr Johnson's reticence) had still occasion to protest: "an inquisitiveness into the minutest circumstances and casual sayings of eminent contemporaries is indeed quite natural; but so are all our follies." It does not further our appreciation of *Hamlet* to know that Shakespeare left Ann Hathaway his second-best bedstead. On the other hand, it makes a great difference to be acquainted with such details of a poet's life as illustrate his spiritual development; and here, unfortunately, Lucretius fails us. He has no pro-

[1] iii. 57.
[2] There are good remarks on the two personalities of each human mind in E. M. Forster's *Anonymity* (Hogarth Press, 1925).

gressive biography. We do not even know whether
he started as an Empedoclean in philosophy, according to Masson's conjecture.[1] All that we can
infer from the poem is that Lucretius warmly admired Empedocles, who served him as the model
of his work on Nature. Again, as Masson also
suggests, he may speak, in the Fourth book, "as
one who had experience of passionate love, seem-
ingly for one who was not worthy of him".[2]
Possibly, like Catullus, he had such a fate, but it
is a mere hypothesis; we have no authority for the
legend that there was a "Lucilia (Lucilla) wedded
to Lucretius" who "found her master cold".[3]

As to the circumstance of his death, too, we
must curb our curiosity. We might like to know
for certain whether he committed suicide; but
such knowledge would hardly bear on his poetic
development—it has been well said (by J. K.
Stephen) that death comes too late in life to enable
us to enlarge our experiences.

There remains the question whether Cicero
"edited" the *De Rerum Natura*. Here again, Jerome's statement has been doubted, since the
orator, although he mentioned Lucretius with
praise, was definitely hostile to Epicureanism,
which he treated with contempt. Did Cicero dif-

[1] Masson, *op. cit.* p. 57.   [2] *Ibid.* p. 396 *n.*
[3] Tennyson's story appears to be of Renascence origin. See
Merrill, p. 17.

88

ferentiate between the poet and his philosophy?
It would be pleasant to think that he was so broad-
minded; and, after all, his greatest friend, Atticus,
was an Epicurean. Moreover, we learn from a
letter of Pliny that he "befriended poets with
wonderful kindness".[1] Lucretius must have died
before the completion of his work, which he left
unrevised as well as unpublished; and Cicero,
being by far the most conspicuous man of letters
at the time, might naturally have been either invited, or later thought to have been invited,[2] to
publish a work which he admired.[3] Anyhow, he
could not have taken the task of "emendation"
very seriously, for the *De Rerum Natura* is full of
repetitions, misplaced lines or paragraphs, promise
of discussion unredeemed, and other signs of the
author's lack of revision.

The poem, however, must have been given to
the world in much the form that Lucretius had
contemplated, as in the opening of the Sixth book,
addressed to the Muse, he speaks of his work as
running "the last lap of his prescribed course".
But he had not reached the actual goal. The work
breaks off in the middle of a vivid description of
the plague at Athens, based very largely on the

[1] Pliny, *Ep.* iii. 15.

[2] The theory that the editor was not Marcus but Quintus
Cicero has not been widely accepted.

[3] Giri (p. 107) suggests the latter alternative.

account of Thucydides, but also owing much to the medical writings of Hippocrates. While it is just possible that the loss of a proper conclusion may be due to a missing end in the archetype, it is more probable that the poem was cut short by the author's death. Even as it now stands, the Sixth book is longer than most of the rest, so that its close may have been brief. The nature of the close can only be conjectured, but Lucretius was much occupied by the thought of death, and it has been suggested that the poet intended to finish the work, which he had begun by an address to the life-giving Venus, with a description of the deadly power wielded by Mars. The two deities stand for the two principles inherent in all Nature; and the mutual struggle of these equal forces brings in turn the creation and disruption of every animate and inanimate thing.[1]

[1] ii. 573–580.

CHAPTER V

GENERAL PRINCIPLES OF
THE SCHOOL

A book on a poet as poet need not discuss his
philosophy in any great detail. But Lucretius
claims to be more than a poet; he is a teacher of
a system, and cannot be understood without some
knowledge of Epicureanism. The physical system
of Epicurus had already been settled (with a few
not unimportant differences) by Democritus; the
Epicurean Brotherhood had been anticipated by
Pythagoras, if not by Plato. But the emphasis on the
personal "way of life" was a new feature, foreign
both to Plato and Aristotle. The Atomism of
Leucippus and Democritus was purely physical—
the necessary and final result of Ionian speculation, in the course of which all other theories had
failed. Democritus (we know much less of Leucippus) was keenly interested in the nature of
Existence for its own sake, and his moral views
were comparatively of no importance. His "cheer-
fulness" (εὐθυμίη) was no great contribution to
philosophy, except in so far as it anticipated the
neutral state of pleasure at which Epicurus aimed.
Epicurus, on the other hand, really despised physics
as unnecessary, if we were free from "suspicions

about natural phenomena and death".[1] That this
distribution of emphasis appealed to Lucretius, it
is impossible to believe. He seems to revert, in
spirit, to Democritus or—we should rather say—
to Empedocles. As has been argued in more detail,
he was endowed with the poet's eye; and although
that eye could not, in his own words, discern a
Hell, his vision extended over the whole horizon
of the natural world, with "divine pleasure and
awe":

> *his ibi me rebus quaedam divina voluptas*
> *percipit atque horror, quod sic natura tua vi*
> *tam manifesta patens ex omni parte retecta est.*[2]

Such an attitude would be unusual for a man who
studies Nature not for her own sake, but merely
as a basis for framing an ethical system. Indeed,
it has caused some surprise that the poet nowhere
develops his moral creed after the manner of
Epicurus himself in his third letter (to Menoeceus).
He is content to draw his moral lesson in a sporadic
way, when occasion serves and his Muse demands.
On the first-principle of Epicurean ethics—that
Pleasure is the End of all action—Lucretius is of
course quite orthodox. He strikes the note in his
opening line, where Venus is *hominum divomque
voluptas*, but the note is hardly heard again until
the poem is well on its way. Meanwhile, his chief
object was *rerum cognoscere causas*. The first two

[1] K.Δ. xi. and xii.   [2] iii. 28.

books are almost wholly occupied with the theory of Atomism; and it is these books, perhaps, more than any of the others, which have given colour to the mistaken criticism that Lucretius has confused poetry with philosophy.[1]

Yet, whatever his love of science for its own sake, Lucretius seems never to miss an opportunity of pointing the moral by showing how the happy life depends on his reading of Nature. The chief object of Epicurus had been to remove corporeal pain (ἀπονία), and, more especially (as body and mind, or soul, were bound up together), to dispel the terrors of the mind, and so to produce ἀταραξία—that feeling of content and security that all post-Aristotelian Greeks sought to attain. This "calm" the Stoics found in Virtue; Epicurus—to the disgust of the schools—sought for the *summum bonum* in Pleasure. But his theory, so far from being an incentive to vulgar "pleasures", turns out to be a negative satisfaction—the absence of pain. Later critics, however much opposed to the theory, agreed that in practice no fault could be found with the definition. Unlike the Cyrenaic Aristippus, whose "pleasure" was momentary (μονόχρονος), Epicurus demanded a static pleasure—a satisfaction that lasted through life, although he left open a loophole for grosser indulgence by allowing that pleasure must be corporeal. It is, however, on

[1] See, however, ch. i.

93

the absence of pain, as we have seen, that Lucretius almost entirely concentrates.[1]

To the philosopher, at all events, the pleasures of the mind are superior, as being the negation of mental disturbance: "in bodily pain the flesh is tormented only by the present, whereas in pain of the mind the soul is tormented by the present, past and future".[2] All sensation arises from touch —it was inconceivable to ancient atomists that one particle should act on another at a distance.[3] Lucretius is moved beyond his wonted calmness of statement in discussing this first-principle of Atomism, when he lays down this axiom of his creed:

> *tactus enim, tactus pro divom numina sancta,*
> *corporis est sensus.*

Here, as in his certainty that the Universe is too vast for any god to govern,[4] the "unphilosophic" oath stresses the importance of the doctrine.

Pleasure, then, as absence of bodily pain and mental trouble is the keynote of Epicurean theory; but Lucretius only hints at part of the definition which his master had elaborately developed. For example, Epicurus had argued—against the Cyrenaics—that pleasure could be varied; and so a selection between them—a hedonistic calculus, in-

---

[1] See above, p. 17.   [2] Diog. L. x. 137.
[3] ii. 434.
[4] ii. 1093; Lange, *op. cit.* vol. i, p. 308.

volving free-will, results.[1] All pleasure, in itself, is natural and therefore good; it is both the beginning and the end of action (the motive and the completion); but some pleasures are to be avoided because they are attended by pain. The Epicurean division of desires was threefold: pleasures are (i) natural and necessary (drink to quench thirst), (ii) natural and not necessary, which vary the pleasure without removing pain (expensive food), (iii) unnatural and unnecessary (crowns and statues).[2] The best commentary on this definition is the remarkable passage in Lucretius (iii. 31–86), where the fear of death leaves no pleasure unalloyed—*liquidam puramque*—and there is room only for Avarice and Envy, which lead to the horrors of civil war and the insane desire for "statues and fame".

Among the many libels on Epicurus, during and after his lifetime, the most unfair was certainly the scandal which charged him with "good living". Some of his later followers, no doubt, deserved the name of "swine from the Epicurean herd", but Epicurus himself, so far from being an epicure—a Stoic slander—was content with bread and water, and thought cheese a luxury. In this abstemiousness, the philosopher was consistent with his theory of pleasure as the removal of pain, since the finest

[1] *Ep*. iii. 129; K.Δ. viii, ix, where see Bailey.
[2] See Bailey on K.Δ. xxix.

feast could give no greater pleasure than the simplest food. It is interesting to remember that Epicurus had himself suffered from enforced abstinence during the siege of Athens by Democritus of Phalerum in 295 B.C., when famine in the city was so bad that the Epicureans were rationed on a few beans.[1] On the other hand, Epicurus had no objection to luxurious food, "if it should be available",[2] and it was perhaps this indifference which gave a handle to the nominal Epicurean. Lucretius himself was by no means of their number; he never shrinks from the strictest asceticism in food:

> divitiae grandes homini sunt vivere parce
> aequo animo; neque enim est unquam penuria parvi.[3]

Granted that Pleasure is the End of Life, Epicurus had to deal with the question how happiness could be attained. His answer was that life cannot be lived pleasurably without prudence, honour and justice.[4] Of these qualities prudence ($\phi\rho\acute{o}\nu\eta\sigma\iota\varsigma$) is chief—indeed, the other virtues spring from it. But what, precisely, does prudence imply? It is the practical side of philosophy, and shows the real nature of the gods and death, as well as the limits of Necessity and Chance. It is true that against Chance ($\tau\acute{v}\chi\eta$) the prudent man cannot entirely

---

[1] Plut. *Demetr*. 34. See W. Wallace, *Epicureanism*, p. 44.
[2] See *Ep*. iii, 130–1, with Bailey's note.
[3] v. 1118 f.   [4] K.Δ. v; *Ep*. iii, 132, 9.

guard himself; but he finds in it an opportunity of attaining great good—or, if this is impossible, he will prefer to be unfortunate with reason rather than to be prosperous with unreason.[1] To Stoic determinism, indeed, Epicurus was an even sterner foe than to popular religion: as he tells Menoeceus, it would be better to accept myths about the gods than to be a slave to the destiny of natural philosophers; for the former suggests the hope of placating the gods by their honour, while the latter has, in its Necessity, a power which cannot be placated.[2]

It is, of course, just here that Epicurus joins issue with Stoicism; and when even the Stoic Seneca, like many moderns, can draw attention to the likenesses between the two schools—"the same law which we declare for virtue, he lays down for pleasure"—it is important to realise that the differences were fundamental, even if the similarities were practically conditioned by the peculiar nature of Greek civilisation.

In discussing Atomism, Lucretius is confronted with the problem of knowledge. On what grounds are we entitled to make any assertion of belief? The answer is found in the "canonic" which Epicurus substituted for the formal logic of Aristotle and the Stoics. Such philosophical spadework is so patently unpoetic that Lucretius himself, who

---

[1] *Ep.* iii. 135.   [2] *Ep.* iii. 134.

deals so freely with the deductions to be made from the canon, is content to summarise the Epicurean theory of cognition in one or two passages which state it as incontrovertible. Briefly, this theory is that knowledge starts with sensation. As stated in the First book:

> *corpus enim per se communis dedicat esse*
> *sensus, cui nisi prima fides fundata valebit*
> *haud erit occultis de rebus quo referentes*
> *confirmare animi quicquam ratione queamus.*[1]

Lucretius, however, is of course fully aware of the importance of the canonic. The κανών, or Rule, was a metaphor derived from the measures used by the builder; and, in an interesting passage of the Fourth book,[2] the poet develops the metaphor, pointing to the need of accuracy in first principles: the carpenter's rule, the square, the plumb-line must all be straight, if the building itself is not to be faulty.

The application of the canonic is very fully discussed in the Fourth book. Reliance on the senses as the sole criterion of truth is of prime importance to Epicurean ethics, since pleasure and pain can only be known by sense-perception.[3] Nor can one sensation convict another of error; each, in its own province, has the same value. If we are not to trust the senses, the only alternative is

---

[1] i. 422; cf. 699. [2] iv. 513 f.
[3] Epicur. *Ep.* iii. 129: ὡς κανόνι τῷ πάθει πᾶν ἀγαθὸν κρίνοντες.

scepticism. But, if a sceptic says "I do not know", how does he know that he does not know?[1] The argument was valid for the ancient scepticism in the neo-academic school—the very claim of the sceptic is logically false; for it presupposes that he has some certain knowledge, i.e. that he knows nothing.[2]

Sensation, therefore, as such is always to be trusted; otherwise reason collapses, and "all the foundations on which the safety of life depends are ruined".[3] But how are we to account for optical and other delusions? The answer of Lucretius is that "the greatest part of these instances deceives us by the mental suppositions which we ourselves add. For there is nothing harder than to discriminate manifest facts from the doubtful things which the mind straightway adds of itself."[4] In other words, the cause of these delusions does not lie in our actual sensations, but in our judgments about them.

What, then, is the proper function of this mind, in relation to the infallible senses? Epicurus adopted the general theory of the earlier Atomists, that all bodies throw off "idols" or images which travel

[1] iv. 469 f.
[2] It should be unnecessary to point out that the "agnostic" attitude is quite another thing. A modern agnostic does not claim that he knows nothing, but that he has no *data* for a knowledge of certain subjects.
[3] iv. 505 f.   [4] iv. 464 f.

through the air and are perceived by collision with
the organs of sense. These films, discharged from
the surface of the solid bodies, move with astonishing speed, and are therefore of extreme subtlety.
Lucretius begins the Fourth book by pointing out
that his theory of sense-perception really negatives
any belief in ghosts (and therefore in survival after
death), since the images are not truly apprehended
by the mind, which does not recognise that such
simulacra are discharged from the living, and may
survive the dissolution of their bodies. The mind
receives these films through the organs of sense,
but does not always take into account distortions
due to the colliding of the atoms in transit. Lucretius devotes a long passage[1] to the explanation of
various optical delusions (such as that of the square
tower seen at a distance as round); they are due
to the "opinions" which we ourselves add, taking
as seen what has not been seen by the senses; for
there is nothing harder than to distinguish clear
evidence from the doubtful opinions which the
mind adds forthwith. Similarly images may not
be simple, but compound, by the blurring of two
or more images in the course of their passage
through the air: hence the *simulacra* of Centaurs
and other monsters, which have never existed.[2]

So far, it might appear that the mind was a
hindrance rather than a help to sense-perception;

[1] iv. 379–465.   [2] iv. 732 f.

and indeed Lucretius does not explain very clearly
the precise theory of the mental process, as laid
down by Epicurus himself. In answering the question: How is the mind to distinguish truth from
falsehood? Epicurus held that the mind, having
grasped an image by apprehension,[1] makes inferences from sensation; such inferences are not
necessarily valid, but if they are constantly tested
and confirmed by sense-perception, a πρόληψις
arises—a precise notion or "anticipation", as distinct from a mere matter of "opinion" (ὑπόληψις),
which may or may not be true according as it is
based upon sensation. In one respect, this reliance
on the senses and distrust of reason carried the
Epicureans to the most absurd conclusions. In
their attitude towards astronomy they held the
extraordinary view that the sun, moon and stars
were not much larger than they appear to our
senses; indeed, these bodies might even be slightly
smaller.[2] It is fair to add that this childish conception was not only derived from the general
trust in the senses, but was also supported by
evidence (inconclusive enough) of fires on earth;
we cease to feel their heat before they appear to
diminish in size at a distance.[3] But we feel the

[1] On the ἐπιβολὴ τῆς διανοίας see Bailey, *Epicurus*, pp. 259–274,
who discusses this technical term.

[2] Epicur. *Ep.* ii. 91; Cic. *Acad.* ii. 82; *Fin.* i. 20 and elsewhere.
Cf. v. 564–591.

[3] See Bailey, *op. cit.* p. 287.

sun's heat—a proof that distance does not lessen its apparent size. There is another "proof": the outline of the moon is (normally) clear and definite, whereas the outline of a terrestrial light is blurred as it is diminished by distance; therefore the moon has not so diminished.[1]

Lucretius deals with other astronomical problems, in which we need not follow him at length. In some of these (on the rising and setting of the celestial bodies, the light of the moon, the nature of eclipses) Epicurus had given alternative explanations on the ground that as long as a particular reason was not negatived by sense-perception it was possible, "for nothing in phenomena is against it".[2] To dogmatise here instead of having an open mind would be to follow "the slavish devices of the (professional) astronomers";[3] and Lucretius nearly always adopts this suspense of judgment for all such phenomena.[4]

With this conception of astronomy, it is curious that the poet felt so much wonder at the *maiestas rerum*. A sun, no bigger than it looks, a moon, which *may* reflect the sun's light, but may just as well be born every day, stars and planets, mere pin-heads of no significance to mankind—how could all these suggest to Lucretius the *praeclara*

---

[1] v. 579–584.   [2] Epicur. *Ep.* ii. 92.
[3] *Ibid.* 93.
[4] See generally book vi for explanation of thunder, lightning, etc.

mundi natura?[1] How could he feel some sympathy
with the uninstructed rabble, who, looking at "the
heavenly quarters of the great world and the ether
fixed above with glittering stars",[2] believed that
this order of the Universe must be ruled by the
gods? The answer is not easy to give. Perhaps we
may conjecture that it was just this world-order
which led Lucretius to "fear" in his heart—like
many materialists—that blind forces are not enough
to account for the harmony of things. Or else, if
we are to assume that here, at least, the Epicurean
poet was consistent, true to his philosophy, he must
have held that nature was an *adlaudabile opus*, precisely because her wonders could be traced in the
tiny atom as well as in the Universe: sun, moon
and stars were indeed exiguous in size, but their
action and effects were immense. Modern astronomy has made us so familiar with the distance
and dimensions of the sun and stars, that we find
it difficult to realise that Lucretius had far other
ideas of magnitude. He knew how large a part
was played in terrestrial life by the heavenly bodies,
even if he had no modern conception of the solar
system, and indeed fell far behind his own contemporaries in their astronomical guesses.[3]

In practice, it may be added, the "pin-head"
theory suited Epicurus very well; it was an ad-
mirable argument to reinforce his general cam-

[1] v. 157.   [2] v. 1204.   [3] See ch. IX.

paign against superstition. So far from being divine, the heavenly bodies, like the earth itself, were simply atomic, and had no more influence on mankind than the real gods, except for their service of giving light and heat. In a material world, these minute bodies could have no other significance for humanity, either as instruments of divine wrath or portents of fate. A considerable part of Graeco-Roman religion was directly or indirectly astrological, and by showing that the stars are neither divine nor even ministers of the gods, Epicurus removed one of the chief objects on which popular—and Stoic—superstition had fastened.

The full details of Atomism, as explained in the Second book, need not be described in this place. It is more interesting to turn to the Third book, where the atoms are considered in relation to human psychology. At the end of the Second book (991–1022) Lucretius had summed up his conclusions as to the atomic origin of all living things. This is logically followed by a discussion of the nature of life and mind; and the poet makes it clear at the outset that his psychology is but a means to an end—to rid men's minds of fear, by showing that the soul is mortal, and there is no need to dread future punishment. Epicurus took over from Plato the idea of a bipartite soul—of which one part was rational (λογικόν), the other irrational (ἄλογον); but whereas both parts were comprised in a single term (ψυχή), Lucretius used two words, *animus* "mind", and *anima* "vital principle". When their natures agree (as in the mortality of both), Lucretius is obliged to state definitely that, in speaking of the *anima*, he includes the *animus*, "since they are one".

The soul is composed of four elements: of which three are like those of wind (*aura, ventus*), heat (*vapor, calor*) and air or mist (*aer*); but as these are not enough to cause sensation, there must be a fourth essence, of the finest possible atoms, which the Greek Epicureans called "nameless"; to Lucretius it is the *quarta natura*.[1] This quartessence was obviously a makeshift to account for the mystery that a body, in itself non-sentient, can have sensation. No doubt the makeshift satisfied the Epicureans; at all events they did not regard the quartessence as super-material—it is as material as the other elements of the soul. It is nameless, because it is unique, and cannot be compared with any other substance. Mind and spirit, then, are composed of all these four elements of the soul, sensation starting with the fourth element and being communicated with the other three in turn.[2]

[1] iii. 282 f. To Democritus, the soul-atoms are πυρώδεις, "fiery", but this unity was not enough for Epicurus. Lucretius omits the "likeness", calling the atoms simply "wind", etc.

[2] I follow the view of C. Giussani and C. Bailey (*Greek Atomists*) against certain German scholars, who restrict the nameless element to the mind. The passage in Lucretius is iii. 231 f.

This nameless element has always been regarded as the weak side of Atomism, which cannot explain Mind by Matter, however fine and swift the atoms may be. In the nineteenth century, even those who were most in agreement with the ancient materialists—Huxley, Tyndall and Haeckel—were forced to acknowledge that the connection of body and "soul" was an insoluble problem;[1] and modern biochemistry has, so far, failed to throw much light on the origin of life.

Lucretius proceeds: the mind and the vital principle make up one nature in conjunction, but the mind is superior, and is situate in the breast, or parts about the heart.[2] This notion was of course popular, though Anaxagoras, Alcmaeon and Plato had held that the brain was the seat of intelligence; but in the ordinary (Aristotelian) view the function of the brain was to cool the blood. The choice of the heart was due to mistaken observation: the heart beats quicker in any excitement, whether from fear or joy, and the mind was thought to be the seat of passions as well as of reason.[3] The *anima* is diffused throughout the body. This theory, again, was due to mistaken observation—limbs

[1] Lange, *op. cit.* p. 267; Tyndall, *Fragments*, p. 122; Haeckel, *Monism*, p. 47.   [2] iii. 136–160.

[3] Of these, the opinion of Alcmaeon is uncertain; see P. Tannery, *L'histoire de la science hellène²*, p. 221 f. The question was finally settled before the second century A.D. when Galen knew the function of the brain.

quiver for some time after they have been cut
off from the body, and nervous reflex action was
mistaken for the continued presence of the *anima*.[1]
The fact that the body can survive the loss of an
arm or leg gave no difficulty: the vital principle
is distributed throughout the body; and some of
the soul-atoms may be lost without affecting the
rest; the body only ceases to have sensation, when
it has lost the sum of atoms which produce the
nature of the soul.[2]

It is an important principle for Epicurus that
the body holds together (στεγάζει) the soul so that
on the dissolution of the body the soul loses sensation. The converse view was held by the Stoics,
and by those who believed that the soul "informs"
its bodily tenement. To Lucretius, the body is but
a kind of vessel (*quasi vas*) to contain the soul.
A material soul must needs perish with the dissolution of the body; and Lucretius devotes several
hundred lines (iii. 417–829) to the proof that what
is born with the body cannot survive its death.
It is in this passage—together with the following
consolation—that Lucretius rises to his subject,
dispiriting as it may seem to some. His proofs
"have long been searched after, and discovered
with sweet labour"—

> *conquisita diu dulcique reperta labore.*

[1] iii. 119–123, 644 f.
[2] See *Ep.* i. 65 and Lucr. iii. 119 f., 640 f.

It is unnecessary to follow the poet in his many arguments—Munro counted no less than twenty-eight. From any materialistic point of view, his position may be regarded as unassailable : as Bailey sums up, "if sensation can be an atomic movement and nothing more, it is impossible to refuse to accept the conclusion that the soul perishes".[1]

[1] *Greek Atomists*, p. 401.

CHAPTER VI

EPICUREAN THEOLOGY

LUCRETIUS follows his master in holding the existence of gods. Epicurus, in his letter to Menoeceus, had made this belief his first commandment, to be repeated in the beginning of the *Principal Doctrines*. His system forbade strict atheism; in dreams the human mind perceives forms or images of gods, and these forms must be "true", for they occur so frequently as to produce an "anticipation", and satisfy the criterion of reality. A second argument lay in the supposition that no nation is without some sort of religious belief, which Velleius, the champion of Epicureanism in Cicero's *De Natura Deorum*, holds that Nature has implanted in man as a primary notion—a view equivalent to a more modern argument based on the assumed universality of religion. Cotta, the opponent of Velleius, asks: How do you know the opinion of all nations? and the question was pertinent, since even modern anthropologists can hardly give an answer with finality—so much depends on the definition of "religion".

No doubt Epicurus, if he failed to understand the nature of the imagination, had at least an ideal which he wished to see realised in the complete happiness of the gods: "the happy and imperish-able nature knows no trouble itself, nor causes trouble to others, so that it is constrained neither by anger nor favours"[1]—a doctrine made me-morable by Lucretius:

> *omnis enim per se divom natura necesse est*
> *immortali aevo summa cum pace fruatur*
> *semota ab nostris rebus seiunctaque longe;*
> *nam privata dolore omni, privata periclis,*
> *ipsa suis pollens opibus, nil indiga nostri,*
> *nec bene promeritis capitur neque tangitur ira.*[2]

It is here, said Epicurus, that popular religion is wrong: the impious man is not one who denies the gods of the multitude, but one who attaches to the gods the beliefs of the multitude. He was as much disgusted with the Homeric gods as Xenophanes or Euripides or Plato; but he was not contented with mere negative criticism; his theo-logy, as far as it went, was constructive. Euripides had said that the gods "needed nothing"; Epicurus added that they were free from all passions.[3] Lucretius more than once makes the same point, as in his fine apostrophe:

> *o genus infelix humanum, talia divis*
> *cum tribuit facta atque iras adiunxit acerbas!*[4]

It is no piety, he adds, to turn to a stone and to approach every altar, but rather to view all things with a tranquil mind.

[1] K.Δ. i. [2] ii. 646 f.
[3] Epicur. *Ep.* iii. 123. [4] v. 1194 f.

These gods are themselves atomic, but, being immortal, are formed of the finest atoms, and could not exist in any world, whose destruction would involve their own ruin. So Lucretius places them in the *intermundia*[1]—"the lucid interspace of world and world".

Were the Epicureans satisfied with a vague description of their gods as constituted of fine atoms, or did they add to this definition? A theory, first advanced by Lachelier, and afterwards accepted by W. Scott and more recently by Giussani,[2] suggests that the gods have only a formal identity; their matter is continually passing away, in a succession of images or material films, like a waterfall, whose appearance remains unchanged, although the water changes each moment. The theory depends largely on an obscure and disputed passage (Cic. *De Nat. Deor.* i. 19. 49) and cannot here be discussed: it has been strongly attacked by Masson, as implying notions foreign to Epicureanism, which seems doubtful. On the other hand, Bailey (after an exhaustive review of the evidence) comes to the conclusion that Epicurus' conception of the constitution of the gods cannot in its main outline

[1] v. 146 f. Lucretius does not use *intermundia*, which occurs in Cicero (*N.D.* i. 8. 18) for the Greek μετακόσμια.

[2] Lachelier, *Revue de Philol.* (1877); W. Scott, *J.P.* (1883), vol. xi, p. 212 f.; Giussani, vol. i, p. 227 f. See against, Masson, *Class. Rev.* (1902, June and December) and his *Lucretius*, vol. i, pp. 277–283, and vol. ii, App. XI.

have been far removed from the account of Scott and Giussani.[1] Luckily, in this place, we may prefer to follow the reticence or forgetfulness of Lucretius, who does not keep his promise to explain the nature of the gods *largo sermone*,[2] rather than the careful particularity of Philodemus, fragments of whose works *On Piety* and *The Life of the Gods* were found in the charred rolls of Herculaneum. That teacher seems to have been explicit enough: the gods require food and drink, but not sleep (which is eliminated as being akin to death), and they even speak Greek or a language very like Greek—as they could hardly have done if they had been "waterfalls". It is hard to believe that Epicurus himself held these notions; but, after all, they were a legacy of popular superstition. Such anthropomorphic ghost-gods may well have the loquacious privileges of the ghost in *Hamlet* and other Shakespearian spectres, while—even if Epicurus deplored the mythological—Homer's nectar and ambrosia were an obvious analogy for the food of the gods.

Lucretius leaves his gods in the *intermundia*, with no further explanation beyond the assurance that they live in peace and happiness. Among the details which he omits to discuss are such questions as the number and precise nature of the gods. Here our information is to some extent supplied

[1] *Greek Atomists*, App. p. 594; see also p. 443 f.
[2] v. 155.

by Philodemus, who says that the gods are even more numerous than the Greeks asserted, and Velleius, Cicero's Epicurean champion,[1] who invokes the principle of "isonomy", balance or equal distribution. Velleius argues that, if there is so great a multitude of mortals, there must be as great a number of immortals. The forces of preservation must be equal to those of destruction. Lucretius had recognised the value of the principle of equilibrium—derived from Empedocles—in the general world of physics, referring to the counterpoise of life and death:

> *sic aequo geritur certamine principiorum*
> *ex infinito contractum tempore bellum,*[2]

as well as in particular instances of animals, rare in some places and "therefore" common in others;[3] and, more or less logically, he must have thought that this theory applied to the gods. Anyhow, Roman religion, with its immense number of minor deities—the *indigitamenta* or spirits with a single or special office—might have favoured the principle. "It is easier", said Petronius, "to find a god in Italy than a human being"; and the lucid interspaces were no less fortunate.

The futility of Epicurean *dieux fainéants* has been a scandal or a matter of derision; but, viewed

---

[1] Philod. περὶ θεῶν διαγωγῆς; Cic. *N.D.* i. 19. 50.
[2] ii. 573 f.
[3] See generally C. Bailey, *Greek Atomists*, p. 461 f.

historically, there is no reason for either attitude. Early Greek speculation had assumed that the world was formed out of chaos, and the gods were somehow included in this rather haphazard cosmogony. Both gods and men, according to Hesiod, were born from the Earth. Even when Anaxagoras had suggested a creative Mind, and Plato had familiarised Greek thought with the conception of a Demiurge, the difficulty of accounting for a providential government of the world was not easily overcome. In the Platonic *Politicus*, the divine Being from time to time lets go the tiller of the Universe, which relapses into a state of disorder, until the guiding Hand again resumes control. From this casual and uncertain care it was only a step to deny the existence of Providence altogether. Such a denial was, after all, the readiest way to explain both the problem of evil and the magnitude of the world, which no anthropomorphic god could be expected to direct. " Who"—asks Lucretius—"can order the infinite mass, who is able to hold and guide the mighty reins of the Universe?"[1] To the Stoics, of course, the very size of the world was an argument for the directing Mind; and even Lucretius seems to be conscious of the difficulty raised by his own materialism. In the fine passage which has already been quoted,[2] he points to "the celestial quarters of the world;

[1] ii. 1095.   [2] v. 1194 f.

and the ether fixed with glittering stars above";
and allows that a disquieting thought (*cura*) may
well arise "lest perchance there should exist an
infinite power of the gods, guiding the stars in
their various paths". Was there ever a beginning
of the world, and will it ever have an end? There
are storms and earthquakes, too, and lightning,
which strikes the very temples of the gods (ii.
1101)—an old argument—so that the peoples and
proud kings tremble for fear that they have offended the powers of heaven. Thunder and lightning—he explains in the Sixth book—are purely
natural phenomena produced by the clashing of
clouds (here the Stoics agreed); but any system of
philosophy found it a hard task to combat the fears
and ignorance of the vulgar both in Greece and
Rome; and Lucretius, in a rare absence of his
dogmatism, is himself compelled to assign the ultimate cause of natural upheavals and catastrophes
to "some hidden force"—*vis abdita quaedam*—which
tramples underfoot the fine *fasces* and cruel axes of
the proud:

> usque adeo res humanas vis abdita quaedam
> obterit, et pulchros fasces saevasque secures
> proculcare ac ludibrio sibi habere videtur.[1]

This "hidden force" is, however, nothing more
than a manifestation of Nature in her less kindly
mood, when Chance intervenes.

[1] v. 1233.

The gods, at least, are not to blame for evil, just
as they are not the authors of good. How, then—it
may be asked—can such beings, who neither reward nor punish, receive prayer and worship?
The Epicurean answer, as given by Lucretius, is
that ignorance about the holy gods is often a cause
of harm—not, he hastens to add, that they will
therefore take vengeance, but because by such
unworthy thoughts the worshipper will not approach their shrines with a peaceful mind, nor
will he receive in tranquillity the images thrown
off by their sacred bodies.[1] That some effluences
of the gods enter the mind and affect it powerfully
for good is also a definite statement in a fragment
of Philodemus, *On Piety*.[2]

The Epicurean religion, then, was essentially
(like Buddhism) contemplative, a kind of adora-
tion which has even been described as "something
like communion".[3] With this idealism, it is not
surprising that Epicurus was said to have been
devout in all religious observances.[4] Such a reli-

[1] vi. 68–78.

[2] Philod. περὶ εὐσ. (Gomperz), p. 86. See Masson, *op. cit.*
vol. i, p. 285, for other reff. esp. Atticus in Eusebius, *Praef. Ev.*
15. 5. The passage in Epicur. *Ep.* iii. 124 does not seem to suggest
any Epicurean belief that divine images do harm to the wicked.
See Bailey, *ad loc.* The "better" effluences (βελτίονας ἀπορροίας)
in Atticus, *l.c.* need not be pressed to imply that there are "worse"
images which affect the evil man.

[3] C. Bailey, *Phases in the Religion of Ancient Rome* (1934), p. 228.

[4] For authorities, see Masson, *op. cit.* vol. i, p. 284.

gion, however, was bound to be misunderstood, and charges of hypocrisy and atheism were brought against him by Plutarch (who was an enemy), by Lucian (who represents common opinion, though himself a scoffer) and by such Christian Fathers as Origen.[1] But even if Epicurus could look for no direct answer to prayers, we have seen that his reverence was sincere. Auguste Comte exhorted his followers to honour the memory of great men, as the basis of the Positivist religion. Like the Epicureans, who held special meetings on the birthdays of the Founder and his chief supporters, Comte carried his worship of humanity so far as to institute twenty-four festivals in the year, and set apart two hours each day for "prayer"—that is, meditation on certain ideals. Epicurus, who devoted his prayer to gods instead of humanity, no doubt shared the ridicule that afterwards fell on the founder of Positivism from those who had other notions of religion.

But what of the famous prayer to Venus, which is placed in the very forefront of the *De Rerum Natura*? The beauty and poetic sincerity of the original Latin has tempted English poets such as Spenser and Dryden, but a modern version may be pardoned:

[1] Plut. *adv. Colot.* 1112; Lucian, *Zeus trag.* 22, *Icaromen.* 32; Orig. *contra Cels.* vii. 66.

Queen Venus, mother of Rome's Aeneid sons,
Pleasure of gods and mortals, who dost fill
All places that the sliding stars o'erhang
—Earth, the fruit-giver, Sea, the bearer of ships—
Since all things live by thee, and at thy will
Rise to behold the shining of the sun.
Thou comest, and the winds disperse; the clouds
Flee at thine advent, and the daedal earth
Breaks into odorous blooming; 'tis for thee
The face of Ocean laughs, and radiant Peace
Clothes heaven with glorious canopy of light.
So soon as Spring is dawning, and, unchained,
The Zephyr sheds his genial influence,
Fowls of the air, thine earliest harbingers,
Herald thine advent, every heart aflame
With urge of thee, and all the forest things
Frisk in the field, and swim the violent stream,
Drawn by thy beauty. Such desire of thee
Spurs each to follow, whithersoever led,
Till, over sea and mountain, river-flood,
Green plain, and leaf-embowered home of birds,
Thou plantest in all hearts enticing love,
To multiply, replenishing their kind.
For only thou dost guide the universe,
And nothing wins the splendid shores of light
Without thee; since there grows no loveliness
Nor joy, without thee, I entreat thine aid
Fain to indite the nature of all things
To Memmius mine, to whom thou hast given all grace
Always: and so the gladlier crown my verse
With charm eternal.
                              Grant us peace the while,
Lady! and bid the cruel work of war
Slumber and sleep on every sea and land.
Thine, thine is the power alone, peace to bestow,
Since Mars is arbiter of cruel war,

And many a time he sinks upon thy breast
Deep-smitten by imperishable desire.
His comely neck bends back; his greedy eyes
Gaze upward, feeding on thee, and, with his breath
Hanging upon thy lips, he lies supine.
Ah! then, enfold thy lover, holy Queen,
With thy pure body's overshadowing,
Speak tender words, and beg a boon for Rome
—Peace: for amid the ruin of our land
I have but little heart for this my task,
Nor may a Memmius fail his country's call.   i. 1–43

It is at first sight astonishing that the poet who denied any divine interference with the world should have prefaced his work with an invocation to one of the gods officially worshipped by the Romans. That, strictly, Lucretius is inconsistent there can be no doubt; but his precise motives are not so clear. The prayer cannot be a conventional concession to popular belief. Such an inconsistency might have crept into a poem whose author could be unconsciously influenced by memories of a creed which he had outgrown. But the prayer to Venus is obviously planned for its place in the very forefront of the *De Rerum Natura*. It is a preface to the whole work, independent of the special introductions to the several books. Lucretius himself could have felt no qualms about its perfect appropriateness. An allegorical follower of Euhemerus, he simply used the name of Venus to represent the primal force of Nature:

> *quae quoniam rerum naturam sola gubernas.*

He might, it is true, have personified Nature, which he so often regards as an active force as well as passive matter; but, like other Romans, he never quite reached the stage of this personification—the farthest he goes is to say that *if* Nature had a voice, she would use it against the man who clings unreasonably to life.[1] Nature, apparently, had to wait for centuries for her full personification, and then fared very badly, as Claudian could do no more than make her keep the door at the Cave of the Years.[2] Meanwhile, Aphrodite (Urania), in Greece, and Venus, at Rome, did Nature's work efficiently. Poetic tradition, from the Homeric Hymns to Euripides, demanded recognition of Aphrodite as the parent and nurse of all things living. Indeed, his philosophy no less than his poetry would have suffered by the substitution of *Natura* for Venus. As a philosopher, he was at pains to declare that the gods whom men ignorantly worshipped were symbols of natural activities or departments of the world: "If anyone has a mind to call the sea Neptune or the corn Ceres, and prefers to misuse the name of Bacchus, rather than to utter the true name of the liquor, let us allow him to call the Earth mother of the gods, provided that he forbear to stain his mind in real earnest with foul superstition."[3] Such is his *caveat*, to fol-

---

[1] See p. 131.   [2] Claudian, *De laud. Stilich.* ii. 431.
[3] ii. 655 f.

low the magnificent description of Cybele in her triumphal procession. But, as a poet, he draws on the inexhaustible stores of mythology: his identification of Venus with Nature would deceive no ancient reader any more than it deceived Tennyson:

> As the great Sicilian called
> Calliope to grace his golden verse—
> Aye, and this Kypris also—did I take
> That popular name of thine to shadow forth
> The all-generating powers and genial heat
> Of Nature....

The "great Sicilian" had himself identified Aphrodite with Friendship which, with Strife (the Mars of Lucretius), had alternately acted as one of the first principles of world-creation; and in view of the eulogy on Empedocles in the First book of the *De Rerum Natura*[1] it has even been suggested that Lucretius had been an Empedoclean in his earlier life.[2] There is no doubt that Epicurus had studied Empedocles among the early physicists; but that Lucretius himself did more than follow Epicurean philosophy cannot be proved. It is true that the Empedoclean work on Nature was the model of the *De Rerum Natura*, and that Lucretius confines his praise to the Sicilian, while blaming Heraclitus and refuting Anaxagoras. But admiration need not imply pupilage.

[1] i. 705–733. [2] Masson, *op. cit.* vol. i, p. 57.

There were other reasons for the choice of Venus, besides her presence as one of the pair who, by the principle of equilibrium (isonomy), wove and unwove the texture of the Universe. Scholars have often remarked that the Memmii had taken over her cult from Sulla and that coins of the Memmian gens bear the head of Venus crowning Cupid. It is possible, too, that Lucretius may have seen a group of statuary representing the goddess with her lover, Mars.[1] Like Catullus, he was certainly influenced by plastic or pictorial representations; his fine account of the goddess of Spring and her train was probably suggested by a painting, just as, in its turn, that passage inspired Botticelli's *Primavera*. There may be "a strange contrast between the Venus of the opening lines, the world-spirit filling earth and air, and the mythological Venus depicted in the close of the same paragraph in a love-scene with Mars".[2] Strange, perhaps, to modern minds; but long before Lucretius, allegory had been brought in—or dragged in—to explain personification, and a Greek or Roman poet would pass easily and insensibly from one conception to the other. Even Empedocles had scarcely gone beyond the philosophic stage, in his Love and Strife, though he sometimes identifies φιλία with Aphrodite. Lucretius, being no profound or original

[1] So Martha, *op. cit.* p. 67 and App. p. 358.
[2] Masson, *op. cit.* vol. ii, p. 136.

philosopher, but a great poet, removes the two world-principles from the bare category of a philosophic concept, and extracts their poetic essence. In the *De Rerum Natura* he speaks with two voices; and, at the beginning, the poetic voice—too often, perhaps, repressed by the Epicurean—breaks into a triumphal overtone.

CHAPTER VII

THE FEAR OF DEATH

I

I F the soul is mortal and the gods do not concern themselves with human affairs, it followed that all Greek religion, from Homer to Plato, was mistaken. To Epicurus, there was nothing to hope for, after death, but there was also nothing to fear; and it seemed that the fear of survival far outweighed the hope. Probably the average unphilosophic Greek had hardly advanced beyond the shadowy Homeric after-world, in which Achilles had complained that it was better to be a living serf than king among the dead. No doubt the Mysteries (whether Orphic or Eleusinian) gave promise of a happy existence in Hades for the initiated; but against this hope there must be set the thoroughly Greek conviction that life, divorced from the body, was either un-thinkable or at least worthless, even if the punish-ment of an Ixion or a Tityos were exceptional, reserved for those who had specially offended the malevolent gods.[1] For Epicurus was not alone in denying a Hell. The Stoic Chrysippus ridiculed the Platonic myths of reward and punishment,

---

[1] On Greek (especially Orphic) beliefs in a future life, see W. K. C. Guthrie, *Orpheus and Greek Religion* (1935), ch. v.

holding that the hell of a wicked man was his own
life on earth. We do not know how far Epicurus
thought it necessary to combat the popular views
about a Future Life; but it seems improbable that
he took them very seriously: all "myths" were to
be disdained by the philosopher, and superstitions
about the Hereafter were part of this δεισιδαιμονία.

But Lucretius is in real earnest; and the question
has often been raised whether he not only goes
beyond the warrant of his master but behind that
of ordinary Roman belief in the after-world. Unfortunately, it is very difficult to find out the
precise nature of this belief. On the one hand,
there is the cult of ancestors (the Manes) which
was certainly almost universal, and, if vague and
negative, implied a more or less happy state in the
spirit-world; on the other hand, the trend of
Graeco-Roman thought was towards a doubt or
denial of a future life. Even the Stoics, for the
most part, refused to accept the doctrine, except
for illustrious men, whose souls might survive until
the final catastrophe of the world, when they would
be resolved into the universal soul. Platonism alone
maintained the teaching of the *Phaedo*. Lucretius,
therefore, had good philosophic company in re-
fusing to accept the theory of survival, even if
some, at least, of his arguments were specially
Epicurean. His case was still stronger, when the
fear of Hell was added to the hope of a modified

equivalent of the Christian Heaven. The philosophers and poets (except Virgil in the Sixth book
of the *Aeneid*) were scornful about such notions:
Cicero dismisses the belief in Hell as an old-wives'
tale: later, Pliny the Elder energetically protested
against the idea of any survival, and Juvenal is no
less contemptuous about the Manes and the sub-
terranean realms.[1]

Why, then, does Lucretius deny, with so much
vigour and insistence, not only the survival of the
soul, but the more repellent doctrine of Hell? Is he
merely fighting a shadow? It is often suggested
that the poet was highly strung, or even mentally
abnormal, so that the fear of punishment after
death had become an obsession. This may possibly
be true—if we allow Dante and Milton to have
been similarly obsessed, not to mention many per-
fervid Believers in Victorian Britain. But we need
look no further than to Italian—if not Greek—
superstition to account for his vehement denials.
Even Plato, in the *Republic*,[2] had fallen a victim
to the popular belief in a Hell; and, nearer home,
Lucretius could have found still more savage super-

---

[1] Cic. *Tusc.* i. 21. 48; Seneca, *Ep.* 24. 18; Pliny, *N.H.* vii. 55;
Juv. xiii. 48. See on the whole question Boissier, *Rel. Rom.*
i. 300; S. Dill, *Roman Society to M. Aurelius*, p. 499 f.; Masson,
Lucretius, vol. i. p. 401 f.; Warde Fowler, *Religious Experience of the
Roman People* (1911); Cumont, *After Life in Roman Paganism* (1922);
C. Bailey, *Phases in the Religion of Ancient Rome*, p. 219 f.

[2] x. 615 f.

stitions. Etruscan religion, in particular, was much occupied with the tortures of the underworld, and Tuscan tombs were grimly decorated with paintings of Charun engaged in punishing the souls of sinners. As Conway remarks: "It was not a pleasant thing in Etruria to fall into the hands of Death."[1] That this idea had permeated to other parts of Italy is clear from the evidence of Plautus, who makes a slave describe how he has seen many pictures of torments by the Acheron.[2] Lucretius may have passed a childhood in which all these Etruscan and Italian superstitions were vividly engraved in his own mind, and he may have over-estimated the influence of the old-wives' tales on the minds of his countrymen, even the most uneducated. But we must remember that the Greeks themselves pointed to the awful warning of Sisyphus and other Homeric sinners. Epicurus could hardly have failed to improve their occasion.

If, however, Lucretius exaggerated the views of his master, it may be noticed that his own views on future punishment have often been themselves exaggerated by his modern enemies or apologists. As a matter of fact, the emphasis on Hell in the Third book is more apparent than real. The poet

[1] R. S. Conway (*Ancient Italy and Modern Religion* (1933), p. 62), who prints several pictures illustrating these tortures. See also F. de Ruyt, *Charun, démon étrusque de la mort* (1934).

[2] Plaut. *Captivi*, v. 4. 1 (998).

is not so much concerned to refute a popular belief as to point its moral, if rightly understood. The section which deals with Acheron amounts to less than fifty lines,[1] and its true importance is not merely to reject the superstition of punishment in the after-world, but to explain the myth as having only an "earthly meaning". It is an allegory on human fears and desires, or frustrated ambition, or dissatisfaction with the simple pleasures of life. There is plenty of punishment in real life, says Lucretius, and even if physical torture is not to be dreaded, there still remains *mens sibi conscia*, the conscience—to Lucretius a formidable deterrent, since only the just man is free from fear,[2] although it is true that the conscience is ultimately due to no motive more ideal than the fear of being found out. Epicurus, at least, acknowledged that a simple answer was difficult to the question: Will the wise man transgress the laws, if he knows that he will escape detection?[3] As Epicurus of course believed that laws were man-made, he may well have held that certain laws, at least, could be neglected without violation of "justice".[4] But, since justice itself had no higher authority than self-interest, it is difficult to see how he could have supported the claims of this δίκη, if they conflicted with indi-

[1] 978–1023.   [2] K.Δ. xvii. Cf. Lucr. v. 1151 f.
[3] Epicur. Fragm. B 2 Bailey.
[4] K.Δ. xxxiii and xxxiv.

vidual pleasure. Perhaps there was some room
for doubt in cases of casuistry from the fact that
Epicurean justice arose from a *mutual* compact.
Anyhow, Lucretius himself dismisses the question
very simply, with no suggestion of altruism: there
is no security that your sin will not find you out,
whether you talk in your sleep or in delirium—a
matter-of-fact explanation of the conscience on
which Stoics and poets like Juvenal were moved to
an almost Christian fervour.[1]

II

Lucretius, then, is less concerned with Cerberus and
the Styx than with the longing for immortality
(τὸν τῆς ἀθανασίας πόθον), which his master had
deprecated. The "Consolation" (for so it may be
called) follows the numerous arguments for the
soul's mortality in the first half of the Third book.
It begins with a poetic amplification of the theme
"Death is nothing to us: for all good and evil are
in sensation, and death is the loss of sensation".[2]
In a translation of the poet's own words, the theme
becomes as follows:

> To us, then, death is nothing, and no whit
> Concerns us, since the nature of the mind
> Is proven mortal. As in bygone days

[1] v. 1158 f. Seneca, *Ep.* 97. 15, and many others dissent from
Epicurus.
[2] Epicur. *ad Menoec.* 124.

We felt no trouble, when the Punic host
Came from all quarters to the clash of war
And the whole world shook with the battle-din
Reeling 'neath heaven's high shores, and there
    was doubt
Which of the two should win the imperial prize
—All human power by land and sea : even so
What time we live no more, when body and soul,
That make the single Being, shall be divorced,
'Tis sure no sense of any happening
Can stir us from the nothingness of death,
Though earth and sea be mingled, sea and sky.
Nay, even suppose the nature of the mind
And power of soul, rent from the body, could feel,
Yet nought is that to us, whose being is one
In partnership and marriage of the twain.[1]

Lucretius goes on to point out the inconsistency
of one who troubles himself over the disintegration
of his body. After all, he says, it is no worse to be
mangled after death by wild beasts than to be
cremated or buried under a heavy slab. Then the
poet changes his tone, for the moment, from sar-
casm to pathos, in the famous lines put into the
mouth of those who cling to life :

> *iam iam non domus accipiet te laeta, neque uxor*
> *optima, nec dulces occurrent oscula nati*
> *praeripere, et tacita pectus dulcedine tangent.*[2]

The thought is common to Epicureanism—and to
humanity; but nowhere has it found more dignified
and poetic expression than in Lucretius, with his

[1] iii. 830 f.   [2] iii. 894.

quiet conclusion: What cause is there for the
eternal mourning of survivors, if all comes to sleep
and rest? It has been said that the poet "stifles
the cries of the heart which touch and annoy him,
having no consolation to offer".[1] But there is
surely here no "stifling of the heart". Lucretius—
or the *anti-Lucrèce chez Lucrèce*—feels for the weaker
brethren, even if he knows it to be his duty to tell
them the truth. Anyhow, the mood of sympathy
soon passes, succeeded by sterner accents: Nature
herself is half-personified, and would ask the mortal
why he weeps at the thought of death: "thou fool,
if thy former life has been happy, why not be content to depart like a feaster full of life? If, however,
thy life irks thee, why seek to add more to its
unhappiness?" Nature has nothing fresh to offer—
eadem sunt omnia semper.[2] Better men than thou
have died—King Ancus, the Scipios, Democritus,
Epicurus himself. Finally, there comes a passage
of supreme satire, in which Lucretius urges the
study of natural philosophy for those who are bored
with their lives, like the young noble leaving his
great house, soon to return, yawning, because he
finds nothing better in the country.[3]

The poetry of the Third book cannot be questioned, although there have been many to complain that the "Consolation" does not console.

[1] Martha, *op. cit.* p. 142.
[2] iii. 931 f.   [3] See ch. I, p. 30.

Its arguments are far-reaching, and seem to have satisfied philosophers like Montaigne, but they hardly cover the whole ground. As Santayana points out, it is not enough to say, While you still live, death is absent; when you are dead, you are so dead that you cannot know you are dead and so regret it.[1] Epicurus, in fact, is weak in his psychology. For, in the first place, the ordinary man does not, perhaps, fear death in the abstract so much as the painful process of dying. The sentiment of Cicero (or Ennius) may still hold good:

> *Emori nolo, sed me esse mortuum nihil aestimo.*[2]

It has often been remarked that we need have no apprehension in doing what many millions have done successfully before us. Lucretius himself makes this point in his reference to "better men" like the Scipios and even Epicurus; but he fails to take into account the natural instinct of self-preservation which animals—the *specula naturae*—share with men. This instinct is, perhaps, scarcely capable of analysis; but its existence, however we may explain it,[3] should not have been neglected by Lucretius, who well knew, as much as the Stoics,

[1] G. Santayana, *Three Philosophical Poets* (1922), pp. 50–57.

[2] Cic. *Tusc.* i. 8. 15.

[3] In a letter to John Morley (1883), T. H. Huxley wrote: "It is a curious thing that I find my dislike of extinction increasing as I grow older and nearer the goal." Many older men will agree.

132

the importance of this primary law; but it was no part of his philosophy to argue against his own case. He really feared life more than death. If he had been quite consistent he might have carried this fear of life to an ideal of complete asceticism, instead of halting between the theory of indulging in pleasures and the practice of being moderate in their indulgence. The fear of death could only be eradicated by the extinction of all that makes life worth living. Here Epicureanism was a compromise: it had no place for certain vices such as ambition and luxury; but its simple pleasures were sufficient to make a banquet of life, which few of the feasters could be expected to leave with willingness. So Lucretius prefers to concentrate on the monotony of the banquet.

The "Consolation" is yet further inconclusive. In his denial of altruism, as a force not only operative in the family, but in a much wider social sphere, Epicurus had altogether neglected the human feeling which causes men to deplore death, as putting an end to their sympathies and their interests in life. Dr Johnson—to take a classical English example—acknowledged "with a look of horrour that he was much oppressed by the fear of death". He did not give his reasons, but, although these may be partly connected with his ill-health and "morbid melancholy"—Epicurus shared the first disability, but not the second—the chief reason was probably Johnson's strong intellectual vitality coupled with an abiding interest, not only in his own affairs, but in those of his friends and the world at large.

Epicurus had done his utmost to suppress this feeling. No doubt, like Lucretius, he was superior, in some respects, to his creed. Patin's phrase—*l'anti-Lucrèce chez Lucrèce*—might be applied with a change of names to the Founder, with the difference that, whereas the inconsistency of Lucretius was partly due to his poetic genius, Epicurus himself could not wholly reconcile his philosophy with his humanity. He left a will which gave explicit instructions about the care of his slaves and other dependents; but on all this very human side his creed was unconsciously in abeyance.

Lucretius—to judge from his poetry—made a far less willing surrender of his life. Indeed, it might be plausibly argued that he would not have been likely to commit suicide precisely for this reason—his life-work was unfinished, his book still incomplete; and no writer hurrying to run the last lap of his race would beg his Muse to point out the goal, and then, by his own volition, would fail to reach it.[1] Every book of the *De Rerum Natura* bears witness to his vehement energy. In his own words, he was ready "to bear any labour and lie awake

[1] G. Giri, *op. cit.* p. 12 f., who rejects the tradition of suicide, points to Lucretius' hope of glory, i. 922.

through quiet nights". This ardent spirit is not least apparent in the tone of the "Consolation", where—it has often been remarked—the poet is in strong contrast with his master. The letter to Menoeceus suggests that Epicurus had no strong hold on life, however desirable (ἀσπαστόν) it may be. Swinburne has not unfairly expressed these negative feelings of the Greek philosopher, in the famous lines:

> From too much love of living,
> From hope and fear set free,
> We thank with brief thanksgiving
> Whatever gods may be,
> That no life lives for ever....

But *The Garden of Persephone*—even less than Fitzgerald's version of Omar Khayyam—is no true exposition of Lucretius himself. The apathy of a wearied hedonist is far removed from the fervour of the Roman poet, who berates and belabours the "shrinking coward" unsatisfied with his share in the banquet of life. So far from merely showing a "proud desperate fortitude"—in Sellar's words [1]— the poet seems rather to hold a legal brief for Death. He turns Nature—*si vocem rerum natura repente mittat*—into a prosecuting counsel demanding sentence on the "aged fool" who clings to living,[2] as though life were not given to all in

---

[1] *Roman Poets of the Republic*, p. 296.
[2] iii. 955. The propriety of the legal metaphor in the mouth of Nature, as a Roman advocate, is obvious.

THE FEAR OF DEATH

usufruct, to none in fee-simple. The proceedings
of a Roman law-court were of course conducted
according to the strict rules of rhetoric; and here,
if anywhere in his poem, Lucretius might be pardoned for descending—or, as a Roman would have
thought—for ascending to forensic language and
methods. Even Virgil did not disdain to write his
speeches in conformity with rhetorical art.[1] It has
recently been suggested that Lucretius composed
the whole of his Third book in accordance with a
rhetorical thesis: he started with an *exordium*, the
praise of Epicurus, and followed this with the
regular parts of an oration—*confirmatio* and *refutatio*,
ending with a long peroration (830 f.) to prove
that "death is nothing to us".[2]

Without agreeing to every detail in this interesting essay, we must at least acknowledge that
Lucretius, so far from being hampered by "the
rules", found them a help to his inspiration, like
Virgil, and unlike Lucan, on whom they merely
tyrannised.

III

After considering the theology as well as the ethics
of Lucretius, we are in a better position to discuss
the question, so often raised, Was the poet a pessi-
mist? In a philosophic definition of the word,

[1] See further, *Roman Poetry*, pp. 17–25.
[2] E. K. Rand in *Revue de Philol.* (July, 1934), pp. 243–266.

"pessimism" is a name for the doctrine that "this world is the worst possible or that everything naturally leads to evil".[1] No Epicurean—certainly not Lucretius—could be called pessimistic in this sense: for, if the ordinary man was more or less unregenerate, the Epicurean, almost as much as the Stoic (though for very different reasons), prided himself on the benefits derived from his own philosophy. Even although human nature were recalcitrant, and all its evils could not be pulled up by the roots, still education (*doctrina*) was so powerful that it left few traces of our original depravity, and there is no hindrance to our living a life worthy of the gods.[2] This is optimistic enough for any philosophy or religion; and if the view is originally Platonic,[3] most modern educationalists (and criminologists) can only regret that they hardly share Plato's hopeful view of human nature.

But, in one of its commonest and loosest meanings, pessimism is often identified with sadness or "melancholy", and the *De Rerum Natura* has been condemned as expounding a melancholy creed. In particular, Martha devoted a whole chapter (IX) to the *tristesse du système*, although he allowed that if Epicureanism is "sad", Lucretius was perfectly satisfied with its doctrines, and wanted nothing

[1] *Oxford Dictionary*, s.v.
[2] See the important passage, iii. 307–322.
[3] Plat. *Rep.* 424a, *Laws* 766a.

137

better. But what of the system itself? No doubt many Stoics, with other religious people, have complained that Epicurus left no room for the providential government of the world. Lucretius is eloquent on the subject:

Yet, were I ignorant of primordial seed,
The heaven itself would add one argument
To many a proof, and I should dare affirm
A Providence no wise prepared for us
Nature; her imperfections stand confessed.
Of earth encircled by the broad sweep of sky,
One greedy part the wild beasts claim, in mountain,
Or forest; rocks cover it, marshy wastes,
And ocean that estranges land from land.
And nigh two halves are wrested from our use
By torrid heat, perpetual cold; the fields,
That still remain, would soon be choked with weeds
—Nature's own work—were there no human toil
Opposing, under stress of very life
To groan at the labouring hoe, to break the ground
With straining plough. Did we not turn the clods
For fruitfulness, and urge the soil for birth,
No plant would issue toward the liquid air
Spontaneous; even so, there comes a time
When all whereon we labour, in leaf and flower
Perfect, is parched by the insupportable sun
Or marred by rushing rain and icy frost
Or vexed by onset of the violent wind.
And further, why does Nature breed and rear
Wild beasts to devastate humanity
By land and sea? Why, in the train of the year
Follow diseases? And Death immature
Stalks? Yea, and like a seaman cast ashore
A child lies naked, speechless, impotent

To live unaided, when he sees the light,
Eject by Nature from his mother's womb,
Wauling and whimpering, even as well beseems
One whom so many a pain awaits in life.
But sheep and cattle thrive, and many a beast,
And want no rattles, nor any sweet low voice
Of crooning nurse; nor, with the changing years,
Seek they a change of raiment; need of arms
They know not, nor of battlements to guard
Their own; for Earth herself and Nature's art
Give all things, and all they are satisfied.

v. 195–234.

The last part of the indictment was, or became, common form for philosophers who have belittled the lot of man, and Lucretius need not here be singled out for pessimism. Nor can he be blamed for stating so obvious a fact that a large part of the earth is uninhabitable, or that the earth itself is doomed—a fate on which Stoics, early Christians and modern astronomers have agreed, even if present-day science does not support the belief in the decay of the earth on which Lucretius insisted.[1] So far indeed from being "profoundly melancholy", as he is so often called, the poet has simply stated the facts of life—and death—without undue stress on their sadness. Of course, like all poets (and all human beings) he has his moments of gloom, but his *surgit amari aliquid* does not apply to himself but to those outside the Epicurean fold. It is these unfortunates whom he has chiefly in

[1] ii. 1150 f.

mind, when he utters his plaintive cry: *nequidquam*, whose application Fitzgerald, the translator of a really pessimistic poet, seems rather to have mistaken in writing "I had always observed that mournful *nequicquam*, which comes to throw cold water on us after a little glow of hope".[1] Fitzgerald did not realise that hope burned bright enough for the Epicurean, in spite of all the drawbacks due both to his human nature, and to the *vis abdita quaedam*—the inscrutable power of chance or luck which upsets human calculations.

The ancients, and especially the Stoics, were not backward in criticising the rival sect, but among their accusations, the supposed sadness of the Epicureans was conspicuously absent. Roman Stoics, indeed, could hardly complain on this ground, for their own creed was so grave and austere that a charge of pessimism against Epicurus would have been ridiculous, even if such documents as the hymn of Cleanthes and the work of Epictetus suggest an optimistic view of the universe.[2] The Porch shared with the Garden many of the beliefs—or disbeliefs—that seem to some moderns most unhappy. Few of the Stoics, as we have seen, could have felt any confidence in personal survival after

[1] E. Fitzgerald, *Works*, 3. 285. For *nequidquam* referring to the vain efforts of the non-philosophic, see iv. 464, 1133; v. 1271, 1313, 1332; more general, ii. 1148; v. 1231.

[2] See R. D. Hicks, *Stoic and Epicurean*, p. 14 f., who quotes Dr Adam's fine translation of Cleanthes.

death, except, perhaps, for the wisest or greatest
of men. Their hold on life itself was much weaker
than we find among the Epicureans: suicide—as
has often been remarked—was a frequent refuge
for the Porch, whereas it was comparatively rare
among its rivals, no doubt owing to their Master's
mislike of self-destruction.[1] Lucretius does not
omit the well-known paradox about those who
kill themselves "from fear of death". But the
chief source of Stoic gloom lay in their determinism,
which Epicurus (however unscientifically) had rejected. To co-operate with the gods, to prefer
being led, rather than dragged, by fate,[2] may be
magnificent, but the creed must have seemed de-
pressing to Epicureans, if not to an Epictetus or
a Marcus Aurelius.

There is, however, one feature in the belief of
Epicurus, which the ancients failed to notice, but
which moderns have sharply criticised: the apathy
of the school.[3] It is true that the Stoics, too, prided
themselves on their "imperturbability", but this
ἀταραξία did not prevent them, in theory, from
sharing the councils of kings and emperors, and
taking a full share in such political life as was
possible for a private citizen. Epicurean "calm"

[1] Diog. L. *Life*, 119; Seneca, *Ep.* 24. 23; Lucr. iii. 79. Epicurus,
however, did not actually forbid suicide; see Bailey on fragm. ix.
[2] p. 76.
[3] See Martha, *op. cit.* p. 333 f.

went much further, and must be read in the light
of the motto λάθε βιώσας "live unseen". Seneca
puts the difference between the practice of the two
sects very clearly: *Epicurus ait: non accedet ad rem
publicam sapiens, nisi si quid intervenerit. Zenon ait:
accedet ad rem publicam, nisi si quid impedierit.*[1] It is
in this inaction that moderns have long felt the
real defect of Epicureanism to lie. Such an attitude may have been tolerable or even praise-
worthy during the troublous times of the late
Republic—still more in the Empire; but quiescence
seems strangely out of date at the present day,
when we have gradually learned that the claims
of society are superior to a mere convention *nec
laedere nec violari*. The social contract was but a
poor equivalent for the Stoic altruism, which led
to Roman law in its highest development, as well
as to the noble theory of human brotherhood—a
conception far exceeding the narrow circle of Epicurean Friends, even if we must admit that the
Roman interpretation of Stoic brotherhood was
practically confined to the Roman world, taking
little account of slavery and other blots on that
civilisation.

[1] *De Otio*, 3. 2.

CHAPTER VIII

I

THE ORIGIN OF LIFE

THE Fifth book may be called the coping-stone of Epicurean philosophy. In it, Lucretius sums up the main results attained in the previous books—dealing with cosmogony, the denial of Providence, the mortality of the soul and its relation to the body, the evidence of the senses in connection with astronomy; and he then proceeds to the origin of life in our own world, concluding with his famous account of primitive man. The *De Rerum Natura* might well have stopped with this book, for the Sixth (as we have it) adds little to the sum-total of Epicureanism, beyond an account of certain phenomena in Nature or Man, discussed on materialistic lines to the exclusion of all divine influence.

After inorganic nature, it remained for the poet to show how living things sprang from earth, and how men began to use speech and to acquire civilisation. The origin of life itself had been discussed for centuries before Epicurus, who seems to have been eclectic in his choice between the more or less crude speculations of the Ionians and other philosophers from Anaximander to Aristotle.[1] Of early thinkers—or guessers—Empedocles came nearest to the conceptions of Lamarck and Darwin, although his theory is the merest germ of modern views on evolution. Lucretius follows the great Sicilian in holding that plants preceded animal life, but parts company with him in his curious idea that Nature, in her prentice mood, gave birth to single organic parts which, arising separately, were united at random, and so produced such monstrosities as Centaurs (βουγενῆ ἀνδρόπρωρα). The furthest that the Epicurean would go in meeting Empedocles was to admit "portents"— creatures androgynous, tongueless, eyeless and the like, which perished because they could not propagate their kind.[2] But Scyllas and Chimaeras were plainly unnatural, to be relegated to the region of mythology.[3] In Lucretian biology, there is of course no real anticipation of Darwinism. Whereas modern theories of evolution are concerned with the Descent of Species by structural modification, the Epicureans thought only of those *genera* which failed to survive, through lack of strength or speed or guile, unless, like sheep and

---

[1] I have examined these speculations in *The Anthropology of the Greeks*, ch. III. See generally H. F. Osborn, *From the Greeks to Darwin*, p. 39 f.; A. C. Haddon, *History of Anthropology*, ed. 2. For the περὶ φύσεως of Empedocles, see Diels-Kranz, *Die Fragmente der Vorsokratiker* (1935).

[2] v. 837–854.　　　[3] v. 878–924.

THE ORIGIN OF LIFE

beasts of burden, they were useful to man, and so found protection.[1] Here, Greek speculation stopped; for Aristotle (who preferred to believe that man had no "origin") was confident that species were separate, permanent and unrelated to any common ancestor.[2]

As for human morphology, in the absence of any real theory of evolution, no school of course suggested that the ancestors of man had ever walked on all fours, and that intelligence increased as soon as man attained a bipedal existence and could become a tool-bearing animal. But the power of the human hand was the subject of controversy ever since Anaxagoras had made his great pronouncement that "man is the most intelligent of animals because he has hands".[3] Socrates and the other teleologists naturally protested; among them Aristotle, whose criticism of Anaxagoras was that man possesses hands because he is wisest—Nature always gives an instrument to one fitted to use it.[4] Here Epicurus was severe against teleology; and Lucretius devotes a paragraph in the Fourth book to the "preposterous error" of holding that eyes were made for seeing and feet for walking. A use was found for our organs, but they were not originally meant for that use.[5] It is strange that the Epicu-

[1] v. 855–877.   [2] See *Anthropology of the Greeks*, p. 54.
[3] See more in *Anthropology of the Greeks*, p. 56 f.
[4] Arist. *Partes Anim.* iv. 10, 687 *a* 9.   [5] iv. 822–857.

reans should not have here allowed a purpose for Nature, even if divine Purpose was *anathema*. Their crude ideas on general biology are in stark contrast with their sane conceptions of human development.

From prehistoric biology the poet passes to anthropology; and the question arises whether Lucretius, in his wonderful account of early Man, is more "original" than elsewhere. He has been called, explicitly or implicitly, the first Anthropologist.[1] Unfortunately, except for the *De Rerum Natura* itself, we know little or nothing about Epicurean views of primitive man; but we must infer that Lucretius, here as elsewhere, followed his master. The later Epicureans, as we know from Cicero, made it a point of honour not to diverge from the orthodox tradition.[2] A few details (unimportant in themselves) show that the Epicureans were interested in the origins and primitive history of man,[3] but otherwise we are dependent on the Fifth book for the views of the school; and in this sense we may still continue to call Lucretius the

[1] So E. Clodd, *Pioneers of Evolution*, p. 22; Haddon, *op. cit.* pp. 100–101. Mackail (*Latin Literature*) says "a Roman aristocrat, living among a highly cultivated society, Lucretius had been endowed by nature with the primitive instincts of the **savage**".

[2] Cic. *Fin.* ii. 26.

[3] Censorinus (iv. 9) credits Epicurus with the origin of man from *uteri* (cf. Lucr. v. 808), and Vitruvius (ii. 1) emphasises the discovery of fire, the origin of language and the evolution of architecture.

Father of Anthropology, unless we reserve that
title for Herodotus, as the first collector of facts,
or for Thucydides, who first showed the importance
of these facts in relation to prehistory. Anyhow,
Greek thinkers had for long been exercised over
the rise of civilisation, and Epicurus only chose,
among many theories, the one best suited to his
own scientific position. He denied, of course, the
Hesiodean myths of a Creation and a Golden
Age,[1] in favour of the alternative theory that the
earth had spontaneously given birth to primeval
man. The Golden Age fared no better, being intimately bound up with the belief in a creator, since,
as Guyau remarks, it is difficult to suppose that
an imperfect world would have issued fresh from
the hands of a demiurge, and the problem of evil
is best explained by the theory of decadence—a
Fall.[2] The doctrine of a moral Fall was not incompatible with a rise in material civilisation,
which many Greek thinkers explained as due to
a culture-god or hero, like Prometheus. But, by
the time of the Sophists, rationalism had been
firmly fixed; and even if Euripides followed Anaxagoras in equating Zeus with the Ether, while
Protagoras left the very existence of the gods an
open question, there was a general tendency, at
least in sophistic circles, to substitute a Rise from

[1] Hesiod, *Works and Days*, 109.
[2] *Morale d'Épicure*, p. 155.

147   10-2

primitive savagery for the counter-theory of a Fall. An agnostic like Protagoras could hardly have attached great value to the myth of Prometheus, but he used that culture-hero as a convenient peg on which to hang a sophistic lecture about primitive man, "naked and shoeless, without bed or weapon".[1]

By the end of the fifth century, it is clear that the antitheological view had become "scientific". Aristophanes, in the *Clouds*, laughs at the advanced theories of those who expelled Zeus and made Whirl (Dinos) king in his stead. Even tragedy—consecrated, until the time of Euripides, to the service of the gods—now shows the influence of rationalism. Sophocles, in a famous chorus of the *Antigone*,[2] had suggested that the development of culture was a purely human achievement. He says nothing of any divine instruction; on the contrary, he lays stress on human intellect, which had subdued sea and land, and tamed bird and beast for the service of man. It is true that Sophocles himself was very far from being a rationalist: indeed he represents the high-water mark of Greek religion, purified by the poets from its grosser elements. Behind man, Sophocles undoubtedly saw the hand of God; but, if God gave the power of progress, the actual steps were taken by mankind alone.

[1] See *Anthropology of the Greeks*, p. 38 f.
[2] 333 f.

Greek thought had already travelled some way beyond the stage of the *Prometheus Vinctus*, in which Aeschylus (whatever his own views) referred all progress to a culture-hero. Later tragedy was not to stop at the non-committal position of Sophocles. With the growing disbelief in the gods, there followed a new orientation of anthropology. Critias, a tragic poet who became one of the Thirty Tyrants, held that primitive men lived a savage life until law was invented; and, as crimes still continued, some "wise man" discovered that a belief in the gods might be a further deterrent—a notion to be afterwards perpetuated by the Epicurean Petronius,

primus in orbe deos fecit timor.[1]

The fourth-century poet Moschion also discussed the origin of civilisation, leaving it, however, an open question whether progress was due to Prometheus or to "necessity" or to "long practice", in which Nature was schoolmistress.[2]

Rationalism, then, had been firmly established long before Epicurus was born; and, although his views on anthropology are lost, there can be no doubt that they are faithfully represented in the Fifth book of the *De Rerum Natura*.[3] There, it will be noticed, Lucretius rejects the theory of primitive giants—no doubt because it savoured too much of

[1] Nauck, *Trag. Fragm.* p. 771; Petron. *Frag.* 27.
[2] Nauck, p. 812; Gomperz, *Greek Thinkers* (E.T.), p. 388.
[3] v. 925–end.

the mythical—but, as so often, the Epicurean compromised, believing that the earth in her prime
could bear a larger, stronger, race than was now
possible, when she had become effete.[1] The passage
runs as follows:

But in those days a hardier race, being sons
Of hard earth, lived afield, with larger bones
And stronger, and with mighty sinews framed,
No easy prey to heat or cold, or harm
From novel food or bodily disease.
Through many an orbit of the rolling sun
They still lived nomad; no strong husbandman
Guided the plough, or worked the land with iron,
Or planted saplings, or was skilled to lay
Sickle to the tall tree's decaying branch.
Sun, rain and earth offered spontaneous gifts
Sufficient for their wants; the oak-forest
Gave customary food; the arbutus,
Which now thou seest ripening to red,
Gave fruit still larger, more luxuriant, then;
Other coarse food there was, that well sufficed
Poor man, in the flowery spring-time of the earth.
To slake their thirst, the river and the fount
Called them, as now the thirsty animal tribes
Are summoned by a riotous waterfall
Crashing adown the precipice. Wandering,
Men marked and visited the woodland haunts
Of nymphs, wherefrom they knew that fountains flow
Tumultuously, washing the smooth wet rocks
—Wet rocks, and fleck the emerald moss with spray

[1] See ii. 1144 f. The belief in giants was no doubt supported
by the discovery of mammoth bones; see Frazer on *Paus*. viii.
29. 1.

Or rise and break upon the level land.
Knowledge as yet was wanting, how to employ
Fire, and to clothe the body with skins despoiled
From beasts: in glade and wood and mountain-cave
Man lurked among the bushes squalidly,
To escape the violent lash of wind and rain.

In this description of primitive life on earth, we may notice that the poet is not quite consistent with his account in the Second book.[1] There, he held that, at the beginning, the earth had borne fruits and vines of her own accord—obviously an unconscious reminiscence of the Golden Age, which otherwise he is at pains to refute; for there was never a time when the gods held a golden chain from heaven to earth for the generation of men. But in the Fifth book Lucretius has forgotten the fruitful vines which should have made men happy, and substitutes *pabula dura*—acorns and other berries—which sufficed the needs of "miserable mortals".[2] The discrepancy is perhaps not very serious; but it shows how difficult it was for the most rationalistic thinker to purge himself completely from the myths which he condemned.[3]

[1] ii. 1153 f.

[2] v. 944. *miseris mortalibus* may be a translation of the Homeric δειλοῖσι βροτοῖσι, but Lucretius must have used the epithet advisedly: the rough diet did not conduce to happiness.

[3] Again, in the passage translated above, we may notice the "haunts of nymphs" (*silvestria templa nympharum*, v. 948) in whose existence the poet of course disbelieved.

II

GROWTH OF CIVILISATION

In the state of savagery—Lucretius proceeds—primitive men had neither morals nor law: each individual lived and acted for himself:

> *sponte sua sibi quisque valere et vivere doctus.*

Love was confined to sex-passion, and family life was wanting. Such denial of any altruism was a creed forced on Epicurus partly by the doctrine of Pleasure and partly by the theory of self-sufficiency or, rather, independency of desires (αὐτάρκεια) which, to a greater or less extent, pervaded all the post-Aristotelian schools. The Epicurean, at least, naturally thought of man as himself an atom on a larger scale. Just as each atom was impelled by Nature to temporary collisions with its fellows, so "natural" man preserved his identity and isolation in all his relations with his fellow-men, remaining a unit, even when he seemed to be most gregarious.

The first steps in civilisation, according to Lucretius, were the invention of huts, skin-clothing, the discovery of fire, and marriage followed by family life. In all these, Nature showed the way, leaving progress to gradual experience:

> *usus et impigrae simul experientia mentis*
> *paullatim docuit pedetemptim progredientes.*[1]

[1] v. 1452 f.

152

Epicurus had of course discountenanced the culture-gods like Hermes or Athena;[1] but he was no less at pains to abolish culture-heroes, who were equally tainted with divinity; and the gift of fire by Prometheus or Phoroneus—the former extensively worshipped at Athens—was deeply rooted in popular belief. So Lucretius returns again and again to the accidental discovery of fire by natural agency.[2] At a later stage, metallurgy is assigned to the "casual fire" which Milton—no doubt with Lucretius in his mind—had supposed as its possible origin.[3]

Here, as so often, the poet contradicts the Stoics, or at least the semi-Stoic Posidonius, who had attributed metal-working to one of the "philosophers" of the Golden Age, when veins of ore were melted by a forest fire. Seneca (who quotes this view) dissents, because it seems incredible that a philosopher would trouble about mere utility—*ista tales inveniunt quales colunt*—and Epicurus might well have agreed with Seneca: as there was no Golden Age, there could be no early philosophers.

[1] Lucretius does not discuss the institution of marriage, but he of course rejected the common Greek theory that it was "taught" by a god. He would no doubt have agreed with Crawley (*The Mystic Rose*, vol. ii, p. 32) that "marriage is between individuals and is an individual act". Crawley holds the view that socialistic or communistic marriage is not primitive.

[2] v. 953, 1015, 1091–1104; in 1106 (*rebus et igni*) Lachmann's correction *benigni* is wrong: an early inventor was not inspired by benignity, though he was cleverer than others (1107).

[3] *P.L.* xi. 566; Seneca, *Ep.* 90. 12.

After the poet's account of the first essays in civilisation—the discovery of fire and the institution of marriage, leading to a general softening of the savage mind—the way is open for a reference to the theory of a *foedus* or Contract, best known through Hobbes and Rousseau's later development in the *Contrat Social*. This "concord" was necessary both for the family and for society, whose evolution is traced through kingship to legal magistracy.[1] It is usual to suppose that Lucretius is here thinking in terms of Roman history—the expulsion of the Tarquins and the establishment of consuls; and his references to the Carthaginian war as well as his mention of Ancus and the Scipios show that, even for his material, he was not slavishly dependent on Greek originals. But Athenian history followed much the same course, and the early Epicureans, if not Epicurus himself, may have rested their political theory on the rise of Greek kingship and tyranny, and the growth of democracy.

In the manuscripts the account of human progress is interrupted by a long paragraph on the origin of language (v. 1028–1090), where modern speculation substantially agrees with the common sense of Epicurus. The question was much debated, and it was important for the Epicureans to know that language at first arose naturally ($\phi\acute{v}\sigma\epsilon\iota$), and

---

[1] v. 1108–1150.

was not fixed arbitrarily ($\theta\acute{\epsilon}\sigma\epsilon\iota$), either by a god or a human "name-giver". We have here definite proof that Lucretius followed his master, who discussed the question with much acuteness, coming to the conclusion that language was originally natural, but that later, special names were deliberately given by common consent ($\theta\acute{\epsilon}\sigma\epsilon\iota$),[1] developed from gestures and inarticulate cries; Lucretius himself is mainly concerned with the "natural" stage, and his analogy from the sounds made by animals in their various moods is very striking, and was supported by Darwin: "I cannot doubt that language owes its origin to the imitation and modification of various natural sounds, the voices of other animals, and man's own instinctive cries."[2] It will be noticed that Darwin, like Democritus, attached some importance to imitation; and, in a later passage, Lucretius follows a Greek idea (first found in Alcman) that human singing was a mimicry of birds,[3] while Aristotle reversed the process, holding that many animal habits were copied from man. In both cases the theory of imitation was pressed too hard, as neither Democritus nor Aristotle made allowance for the animal instincts of humanity.

[1] See C. Bailey, *Greek Atomists*, p. 267 f. and on Epicur. *Ep.* i. 75, 76, who quotes Giussani, vol. i, p. 267 f.

[2] *Descent of Man.* Cf. Hor. *Sat.* i. 3. 103; Vitr. ii. 1. 1; Diog. oen. fr. x (William).

[3] v. 1379.

The rest of the Fifth book (after the history of human society) is occupied with the origin—and evil effects—of religion (1161–1240), and then Lucretius returns to his main subject—the sole influence of Nature in the growth of civilisation. Of these paragraphs, the most celebrated for poetic imagination is to be found in his account of agriculture, where *natura creatrix*, as ever, led the way:

But Nature, mother of all created things,
Taught man to sow and graft, herself the type
And first ensample: falling from their trees,
Berries and acorns in due season bore
Thick underwood of saplings. Hence the wish
To engraft the branch and plant the shoot afield.
So, trial on trial succeeding, the sweet croft
Was fostered, and men saw the wilding fruit
Grow tame by tender care; and day by day
The entanglement of woods was driven higher
Up mountain-sides, yielding a place below
To tilth; so might be found on plain and hill
Room for mead, corn, pool, channel and fruitful vine,
So might the grey-green belt of olives run
To mark the bounds of valley and hill and plain,
Even as, to-day, thou seest in varied charm
The countryside adorned with interspace
Of fruits, all sweetly fenced with orchard trees.[1]

Such, in brief outline, is the Epicurean account of primitive man, as imagined by Lucretius. His anthropology has been accepted as the basis of modern science, which starts from the premiss of

[1] v. 1361–1378.

Thucydides,[1] that there are "survivals in culture" and that the customs of uncivilised races are to be explained as vestiges of an original and universal condition. Lucretius follows the method of Thucydides, at least in one observation: contrasting the luxuries with the necessities of life, he points out that man, after all, can exist without corn and wine:

ut fama est aliquas etiam nunc vivere gentes.[2]

It is true that anthropologists, at the present day, have mostly ceased to dogmatise in the manner of Epicurus: it is now thought no business of any scientific worker, as such, to go beyond his proper province by trespassing on the field of metaphysics. As Huxley said, long ago, "anthropology has nothing to do with the truth or falsehood of religion".[3] The way is still open to follow Xenophanes, who could accept the theory of unaided Progress, as part of the divine plan:

The gods never showed mortals everything from the beginning;
But men search for themselves until they discover the better.[4]

[1] Thucydides, i (opening chapters), where Homeric morals and customs are explained by those of the backward tribes in his own day. The germ of the method appears in Herodotus (v. 86), where he remarks that books were originally skins, "as they are still among barbarians". See *Anthropology of the Greeks*, ch. I.　　　[2] v. 17.

[3] Quoted by Haddon, *op. cit.* p. 131.

[4] Xenoph. fr. 18.

Even the Golden Age, although its metal may be tarnished, has found some modern defenders who contrast the real or imagined peace and security of early man with the undoubted drawbacks of civilisation. Lucretius himself, while opposing the belief in a Golden Age, and drawing no ideal picture of primitive times, is quite ready to admit compensation: If, in primitive times, the wild beasts slew their thousands, war and shipwreck now slay their tens of thousands. If many of the savages, seeking for food, poisoned themselves in ignorance, they had not then acquired the art of poisoning others.[1] For a moment, the satirist seems to have taken the place of the anthropologist.

On the whole, the poet seems to favour the life of early society—the progress of civilisation—but not the earliest form as lived by the *silvestre genus terrigenarum*. Here he shows himself to be a true, mediating, Epicurean. On the one hand he is under no illusion as to primitive innocence: although he must have read in Herodotus about such people as the Scythians, he has no belief in the noble Savage. On the other hand he had little respect for the noble Roman. The purple laticlave was an unnecessary exchange for plebeian garments,[2] if not for the skins in which the "earthborn" were protected from the cold. So he compromises (very sensibly) between savagery and a

---

[1] v. 987–1010.   [2] ii. 35; v. 1426 f.

life of luxury. "Progress" had gone too far; he thinks that the mean could be found in the simple country life that survived in many parts of Italy, and he describes, with evident admiration, a gathering of rustics who picnic

propter aquae rivum sub ramis arboris altae.

The Epicureans, like other schools, were anxious to "follow nature", but they refused to define nature with the thoroughness and rude simplicity of Diogenes and his fellow-Cynics. There was, of course, a serious ambiguity in the definition. Are we to follow the specific nature of man, or to co-operate with external Nature? If the latter alternative is intended, are we to call Nature a mother or a cruel stepmother? The Stoics, relying on Providence, could find no flaw in Nature's motherhood, though some thinkers like Pliny the Elder doubted.[1] To Lucretius men are, first, human beings; only in the second place are they the animals which, in Horace's words, crept from the primal earth, *mutum et turpe pecus*.[1] Diogenes had left intellect out of his full reckoning. Between Antisthenes, the first Cynic, and Epicurus, Aristotle had come, to show that human nature is to be explained not merely by origins but by capacity of development. The City was as much part of Nature's design as the Family. Epicurus, indeed,

[1] Pliny, *N.H.* vii. 1 f.   [1] Hor. *Sat.* iii. 99.

was no Aristotelian—the Peripatetic God was too teleological; but this God was, after all, not very remote from Epicurean Nature who, though unconscious, had a purpose of her own. Athens and Rome, if immediately due to "inventors", were ultimately part of Nature.

CHAPTER IX

LUCRETIUS AND MODERN THOUGHT

I

Epicureanism strikes the modern reader as a curious blend of extreme crudity and far-reaching intelligence. The system in all its divisions—canonic, physic and ethic—is, to say the least, so vulnerable to present critics, as indeed it seemed to the ancients themselves, that a doubt may well arise whether the creed does not deserve Macaulay's censure of it as "the silliest and meanest of all systems of natural and moral philosophy". Such a condemnation is of course far too sweeping, even if it is partly justified by the errors into which Epicurus was led by his reliance on sensation. To say that the sun is about as large as it looks is—we might retort on Lucretius—*desipere*, or rather, *perdelirum*. Classical science could do much better than this: as early as the fifth century, Anaxagoras had allowed that the sun was larger than the Peloponnese, and the moon, which had plains and ravines, borrowed the sun's light; and, in the century of Epicurus himself, Aristarchus of Samos not only avoided the pin-head view of astronomy, but came far nearer to modern knowledge in his statement that the sun is seven times the size of the earth, which, with all the planets, moved round the sun. But Epicurus was by no means in the forefront of even ancient science, in nearly every one of its numerous departments, as is amply shown by the achievements of Aristotle and Theophrastus, of Heraclides, Archimedes and Euclid, of Herophilus and Erasistratus. The theory of Atomism may indeed seem to disprove this contention, but, as used by Democritus and Epicurus, it belonged to philosophy, rather than to science. It was a "brilliant guess", evolved to explain the constitution of matter, when other guesses had failed; but it was not proved by experiment, and was supported only by slender and often fortuitous observation.

The Epicureans had practically no hold on Induction, which Aristotle foreshadowed as the guiding principle of natural science. Provided that the supernatural was excluded, it did not matter to Epicurus whether a particular explanation was correct or not. This method—or want of method—is conspicuous in Lucretius; the Fifth book is full of alternative theories to account for a single phenomenon, e.g. the moon may borrow its light from the sun, or it may shine with its own body, or it may be half-bright, half-opaque, or a new moon may be born every day! Indeed, in the number of worlds, *all* these alternative causes may be true. As Lucretius explains, "to dogmatise which particular cause it may be is by no means the part of a man who advances step by step".[1] Since the Epicureans made no change in their theories or methods between the founder and the Roman period, it is difficult to see how Lucretius could make the claim of advancing *pedetemptim*; and, in any case, the indifference towards a single "working hypothesis" hardly suggests the Uniformity of Nature, which is the first postulate of a real science.

The principles of Greek Atomism served and satisfied not only Gassendi but Newton; and so far the connection between ancient and modern physics is no doubt historical.[2] But to look for "anticipations" of the present day in the Democritean system is surely misleading.[3] Science, in the twentieth century, has not merely "broken" the atom, but every conception of the Greek philosopher has suffered with the breakage. Protons and electrons have superseded Newton's hard, massy, impenetrable particles. Physicists no longer speak of mass or solid matter as the ultimate constituent of the Universe. To quote Bertrand Russell: "the belief that matter alone is real will not survive the sceptical arguments derived from the physiological mechanism of sensation. But it has received recently

---

[1] v. 527–533.

[2] See Lange, *op. cit.* p. 255.

[3] Many such "anticipations" are noted by Masson, which are not so much historical as accidental coincidences.

11-2

another blow from the quarter whence it was least to be expected, namely, from physics. The theory of relativity, by merging time into time-space, has damaged the traditional notion of substance more than all the arguments of philosophers....A piece of matter has become, not a persistent thing with varying states, but a system of interrelated events."[1]

To certain scientific minds, objections do not end here. There is nothing in which both Democritus and Epicurus took more pride than the Reign of Law throughout the physical world.[2] The Ananke of these atomists, faithfully emphasised by Lucretius in his many references to the *foedera naturai*, seemed so obvious as to be an inescapable fact, even if Epicurus avoided strict determinism in mankind. But, of recent years, doubt has spread even to this hitherto undoubted presumption: a school of physicists prefer to lay stress on quite a different "law"—of Chance, which has quite a minor place in Greek Atomism, although it is recognised to some extent by Lucretius. According to this view,[3] all seeming regularity in physics is simply a result of many haphazard occurrences. But, against this notion, even a layman may argue that there certainly exist natural "laws", however

[1] Introd. to Lange's *Hist. of Materialism* (1925), p. xii.
[2] See Russell, *ibid.* p. xvi.
[3] For a popular presentation, see E. Schrödinger, *Science and the Human Temperament*, Essays II and III.

much they may need re-interpretation from time to time. Epicurus, then, would hardly have cavilled at this modern recognition of Chance; but, none the less, physical materialism has gone, never to return in its ancient form; and if the metaphysical deductions of Epicurus still remain, the neo-materialist can no longer defend his rationalism by most of the old arguments.

There is, however, one department of Epicurean science which in general has stood the test of time. The anthropology of the school (including the origin of language), as I have tried to show both in this book and elsewhere, is founded so securely that it has become at least the first chapter of its modern development. Not all the merit, of course, is due to Epicurus. Other Greeks—Herodotus, Thucydides, Aristotle—have a full share; but the Founder, or his school, must have the chief credit of accepting and co-ordinating the results of their great predecessors. One cause of their success lay in the fact that these Greeks intuitively grasped the true principle of anthropology—the rise of man from primitive life to civilisation. Whereas the development of Atomism required experiment, in which Greek science was notoriously wanting, anthropologists, at the start of their science, had only to travel and observe. Herodotus fulfilled both these conditions with singular openness of mind. His observation of many peoples taught

him that, if customs differ, the human race is
ultimately one. Thucydides and Aristotle carried
on the Herodotean tradition, in which Epicurus—
though his own work on the subject can only be
inferred from that of his followers—adopted the
same method. It is true that not all his conclusions
on sociology have been accepted. In one particular
case, for instance—the Social Contract—his view
of primitive man has succumbed to modern criticism. Some sort of contract between individuals
was really inherent in the atomic theory, as each
human being, like each atom, was theoretically a
unit, which only coalesced with other units for the
sake of mutual assistance. But, in practice, Epicurus and Lucretius applied the contract to the
later stage of society when men, "wearied of living
by violence, fell of their own accord under laws
and strict enactments".[1]

This condition (whatever its place in the history
of mankind) cannot be upheld. Modern science
has proved that even the lowest savage lives in an
organised community, where the individual counts
for nothing. If the working hypothesis of anthropology is sound, there is conclusive evidence that
the human race never lived in a state of isolation.
Even if we assume (with Westermarck)[2] that man

[1] v. 1143 f.
[2] E. A. Westermarck, *Origin and Development of the Moral Ideas*,
p. 194 f.

166

was not originally a gregarious animal—that he lived in families rather than in tribes—in any case his later gregariousness was natural, not conventional. Here Epicurus failed, as so often, to profit by the teaching of Aristotle, who recognised that no community could arise out of a contract. Even if men were not originally gregarious—and Aristotle held that the isolated family preceded the village—yet the development of the village and city was not conventional, but Nature's purposed End. It is interesting to contrast the view of Polybius, himself by no means an Epicurean, but rather influenced by Aristotle and the Stoic Panaetius. He supposed that in a primitive state, society was nothing but a herding of human beings, like animals, without any conception of justice or virtue. But Polybius escaped from Epicurus by the help of Plato as well as Aristotle: family ties and social relations are natural, though not original; the members of society are in sympathy with each other, and corporate censure or approval of individual acts is the genesis of moral standards.[1] The Stoics, too, were saved from the Epicurean conclusion by their belief in altruism. The fatherhood of Zeus implied the brotherhood of men, although, in practice, Zeus appears to have restricted a citizenship of the world to the "wise".

There is truth—though not the whole truth—in

[1] Polyb. vi. 5–6.

the Epicurean view of a social contract, but, when applied to primitive man, it is a serious anachronism. In modern times, as Maine pointed out long ago, there has been a steady movement from status to contract. Both custom and legislation have tended more and more to free the individual from social restrictions and obligations. In national life, the "emancipation of women" has been the final phase of a process which started with the strict allegiance to the family, by mitigating the rights of Roman parenthood; in wider, international relations, the development of the contract, from tribal treaty to the League of Nations, is the veriest commonplace of History.

II

It may be argued that the value of Epicureanism depends much more on its ethical system than on its physical model of the Universe. The doctrine of Pleasure as the *summum bonum* has no logical or necessary connection with Atomism; and, if the atom of Democritus has completely yielded to science, this is no reason why Pleasure should follow the general rout of materialism. As a fact, however, the Pleasure theory of Epicurus has been almost as badly treated by modern psychology as Greek Atomism by modern physics. Here, again, it must be insisted that Epicurus was by no means in the van of Greek speculation.

The doctrine of Pleasure, as the End, had been
discussed by the sophists, and of course interested
both Plato and Aristotle. But Plato, while ad-
mitting, rather grudgingly, in the *Philebus* that
pleasure might be *a* good, denied that it was *the*
good. Anyhow, he had no sympathy with the
"loves of wild beasts".[1] Aristotle, in the *Ethics*,[2]
re-examined the question, and came to the conclusion that there is pleasure involved in action—
it may be compared with the bloom on a flower.
Although he seems to hesitate whether we act for
pleasure, he cannot be called a hedonist, in any
true sense of the word: pleasure is not identical
with the good, and not every pleasure is to be
chosen; nevertheless some pleasures are to be
chosen for themselves. But hedonism is a wide
term, applied equally to those who believe, with
the Cyrenaics and Epicureans, that, as a psychological fact, men *do* seek their own pleasure, and
those who, with Bentham and Mill, hold that men
ought to seek pleasure (not altogether their own).
A further distinction is drawn between the egoistic
hedonist, who seeks—or ought to seek—his own
pleasure, and the Utilitarian, who seeks—or ought
to seek—the pleasure of others.

The two chief ancient schools of hedonists, with
their pronounced individualism, were of course

[1] *Phileb.* 67 b.
[2] *Eth. Nic.* vii. 14. 1153 *b* 25.

Egoistic. But this lack of altruism has seldom been openly avowed, owing partly to the criticisms of the Stoics, and still more of the (ancient or modern) Puritans. It is true that Hobbes and Gassendi, Helvetius and Mandeville have been quoted as Egoistic; but none of these, perhaps, has been consistent. Some allowance for altruism nearly always emerges from their systems, even when these seem to be most uncompromising. Of the Utilitarians, Bentham came nearest to Epicurus, in holding that man is naturally egoistic, and was only led to altruism by fear. Thus general welfare was identified with individual happiness. The Utilitarian creed—especially that of Mill—gave an ethical turn to hedonism by the wide application of "the pleasure of the greatest number"; and although Epicurus might have claimed that if everyone was an Epicurean, the pleasure of individuals would not be distinguishable from the pleasure of society in general, it is none the less clear that, in theory, the Utilitarians differed widely from their Greek originals.

Another line of approach to the problem of Pleasure was taken by the earliest evolutionists. Herbert Spencer held that pleasant acts are, in the main, beneficial, painful acts, in the main, harmful. Therefore, while all beings aim at self-preservation, indirectly they seek pleasure, and those beings survive which seek pleasure in benefactions. To this it may be replied that a normal animal desires things which are pleasant; in other words, the function of pleasure and pain is to regulate impulse, but it is the impulse, not the pleasure, which is original.

The school of Spencer, in fact, were obliged to emphasise other "ends", such as social vitality. They therefore ceased to be hedonists, i.e. to hold that Pleasure *alone* is the Good. To say that Pleasure, *among other things*, is good in itself, is an entirely different position.[1] No modern school, in fact, could possibly revert to the Egoism of Epicurus, which springs from an ignorance of psychology. He failed to account for any altruistic sentiments; in particular, for self-sacrifice in favour of the young—a natural law even to the lower animals. These "mirrors of nature" were considered by the Epicureans and Stoics alike; but whereas the former were content with the statement that every animal sought pleasure, the latter replied that the young of a species sought health, self-preservation; Pleasure may be involved in the search, but is certainly not the End. Here the Stoics rightly followed Aristotle, whom the Epicureans too often neglected.[2] Their Master, indeed, admitted (however unwillingly) some altruism to temper his rigid Egoism. As Lucretius

[1] See G. E. Moore, *Principia Ethica*, p. 62.
[2] See Cicero, *Fin.* i. 8 f., and the Stoic criticisms in *Fin.* ii. 8–11.

says, "when the woman was united to the man, then first mankind began to soften. Women and children taught them that it was right for all to pity the weak".[1] Such "pity" is really altruistic, however Lucretius explained it to himself; and his emphasis on weakness is at least partly true, since, when the young are helpless, the human species cannot exist without parental care. But *mere* weakness does not completely explain the protective impulse.[2] Plutarch knew better: Even the lower animals would protest against the exclusion of love in family relations.[3] Epicurus might more consistently have dropped the idea of pity, content with the explanation that women and children are a source of pleasure to the man.

The theory of Pity is allied to that developed by Hartley under the name of Association or Sympathy. It was argued that "my pleasure is incomplete without the pleasure of others"; social virtue is the sacrifice of one's own satisfaction to obtain more pleasure for one's self. But this paradox does not meet the real objection to all forms of strict hedonism, that we do not always or often desire "pleasure" but aim at some end which may —or may not—produce pleasure. The truth arises from a verbal confusion, between "pleasure" and

[1] v. 1011 f.   [2] See Westermarck, *op. cit.* p. 188 f.
[3] *De Amore Prol.* 2.

"choice". We speak of a man doing something "at his pleasure", but by this we really mean that he *chooses* an action, but not always a pleasure-giving action. As Henry Sidgwick explained, "throughout the whole scale of my impulses, sensual, emotional and intellectual alike, I can distinguish desires of which the object is something other than my own pleasure".[1] Our impulses are so various that it seems impossible to reduce them to this single stimulus. We often desire an action which is not pleasant, even if there is pleasure in the fulfilment of the action. Aristotle, then, was again nearer the truth than Epicurus.

It is needless to say that the investigation of pleasure and pain has been greatly developed in the psychology of the twentieth century. The language and method may have changed, but the problem remains. In the nineteenth century, the prevalent theory ran that psychological hedonism was a true principle: pleasure and pain determine all conation (mental activity). This view still finds support; but there has also been a distinct return to the principle (ultimately Aristotelian) that living creatures have a "hormic" disposition—a natural tendency to strive towards certain goals.[2] As Dr

[1] Sidgwick, *Methods of Ethics*. See J. S. Mackenzie, *Manual of Ethics*, vol. i, p. 69, and generally J. Watson, *Hedonistic Theories from Aristippus to Spencer*.

[2] See W. McDougall in the *British Journ. of Psychology*, vol. xvii (1926–7), p. 171 f.

McDougall says, while many psychologists have combined psychological hedonism with the hormic theory, others "have adopted a strictly mechanistic view of mental life and behaviour, a view which finds no place for pleasure and pain, or at least assigns to them no rôle". McDougall himself argues for a purely hormic psychology.

Where the specialists are divided, it would ill-become an amateur to rush in; but, on the practical, common-sense issue, we may claim that Epicurean hedonism, however psychologically unsound, was innocuous. Pleasure is, at the very least, an index of vitality; and, as such, it has its significance in the world of morals, if not the very special place which Epicurus claimed. A theory which regards pleasure as the negation of pain does not deserve the obloquy—too often repeated —of Stoic contempt and early Christian idealism. The Epicurean is with us always. We may not agree with his position, but we shall do well to understand it. And no Epicurean is better worth the understanding than the great poet

> *qui potuit rerum cognoscere causas,*
> *atque metus omnes et inexorabile fatum*
> *subiecit pedibus strepitumque Acherontis avari.*

APPENDIX

APPENDIX

The world is too much with us; late and soon,
Getting and spending, we lay waste our powers:
Little we see in Nature that is ours;
We have given our hearts away, a sordid boon!
This Sea that bares her bosom to the moon;
The winds that will be howling at all hours,
And are up-gathered now like sleeping flowers;
For this, for every thing, we are out of tune;
It moves us not.—Great God! I'd rather be
A Pagan suckled in a creed outworn;
So might I, standing on this pleasant lea,
Have glimpses that would make me less forlorn;
Have sight of Proteus rising from the sea;
Or hear old Triton blow his wreathèd horn.

WORDSWORTH.

Illecebris vitae nimium captamur; ab ortu
Solis conterimus vires ad sidera noctis
seu rem perdundo seu quaestum conduplicando.
quantula naturae pars est quam mente animoque,
ut nostram, teneamus: amorem, ignobile donum,
nempe alio nostrum traduximus. hoc maris aequor,
quod gremio ad lunam nudo patet, istaque venti
flamina, quae fundunt nunc quasvis murmura in horas,
nunc concluduntur, florum quasi germina clausa—
haec et cetera sunt animis male consona nostris,
non ea nos tangunt. pro divom numina sancta,
mallem equidem veteri nutriri relligione,
si modo amoeni huius stans inter gramina prati
possem ita naturae spectacula contemplari
quantulacunque, levans aerumnas, dispiceremque
Protea surgentem e ponto, seu tangeret aures
Triton ille senex ubi cornu inflaret aduncum.

APPENDIX

Then, though (too weak to tread the ways of truth)
This age fall back to old idolatry,
Though men return to servitude as fast
As the tide ebbs, to ignominy and shame,
By nations, sink together, we shall still
Find solace—knowing what we have learnt to know,
Rich in true happiness if allowed to be
Faithful alike in forwarding a day
Of firmer trust, joint labourers in the work
(Should Providence such grace to us vouchsafe)
Of their deliverance, surely yet to come.
Prophets of nature, we to them will speak
A lasting inspiration, sanctified
By reason, blest by faith: what we have loved
Others will love, and we will teach them how;
Instruct them how the mind of man becomes
A thousand times more beautiful than the earth
On which he dwells, above this frame of things
(Which, 'mid all revolution in the hopes
And fears of men, doth still remain unchanged)
In beauty exalted, as it is itself
Of quality and fabric more divine.

WORDSWORTH, *The Prelude*.

Tum quamvis effeta aetas vestigia veri
desinat indugredi, et rursum sub religiones
iam cadat antiquas, quamvis refluo ocius aestu
humanum genus ad scelera indignumque revertat
servitium, immersis totis nationibus una,
at solamen erit nobis id nosse quod usu
repperimus; stabitque opulentis vera voluptas,
si deus annuerit, dederitque fidelibu' nobis
hoc donum, ut nostrum liceat conferre laborem
atque illis esse auxilio, nitentibus usque
dum mage firma fides redeat (nam tempore certo
quippe redibit) et e vinclis se solvere possint.
ceu Phoebi ex adyto, nos illustrabimus illis
naturam rerum, divinitus invenientes
perpetuam vocem, ratio quam sancta beavit
et fovit pietas: alii, quod amavimus ante
id discent quoque amare, viamque docebimus ipsi,
ut noscant quanto magis admiranda lepore
mens hominum egregio fiat quam daedala tellus
qua vivunt homines: superaque haec talia texta
(quae, genere humano spem commutante metumque
motibus assiduis, summam stant nacta quietem)
quanta praecellat specie, divinior ut cui
scilicet est fabrica et totius vis animai.

Yes! in the sea of life enisled,
With echoing straits between us thrown,
Dotting the shoreless watery wild,
We mortal millions live *alone*.
The islands feel the enclasping flow,
And then their endless bounds they know.
But when the moon their hollows lights,
And they are swept by balms of spring,
And in their glens, on starry nights,
The nightingales divinely sing;
And lovely notes, from shore to shore
Across the sounds and channels pour—
Oh! then a longing like despair
Is to their farthest caverns sent;
For surely once, they feel, we were
Parts of a single continent!
Now round us spreads the watery plain—
Oh might our marges meet again!
Who order'd, that their longing's fire
Should be, as soon as kindled, cool'd?
Who renders vain their deep desire?—
A God, a God their severance ruled!
And bade betwixt their shores to be
The unplumb'd, salt, estranging sea.

M. ARNOLD.

Quippe hominum vita est tamquam mare: mille
    videmus
Cycladas, incertis quas distinet intervallis
horrisonum magni maris aequor, litoris expers.
sic vivit sibi quisque inter tot milia solus.
insula enim amplexu circumlabentis aquai
tangitur, agnoscitque impostos undique fines.
at si quando altos illustrat luna recessus,
et loca iucundis ver omnia odoribus opplet,
aut ubi sub caelo stellis fulgentibus apto
per nemora effundit dias Philomela querellas,
cuius dulce melos, freta trans resonantia vectum,
largiter accedit diverso e litore litus,
tunc desiderium, cui spes paene omnis adempta est,
antra per et latebras in Cycladas insinuatur:
"nos etenim"—vocem sic insula posse videtur
mittere—"pars olim fuimus telluris: at umor
nunc circumfluit, et vastis nos continet undis.
o si litoribus liceat se iungere rursus!"
quis potis est ardorem illum compescere, ut ortu
iam desiderium cito restinguatur in ipso?
quove iubente perit tam futilis ista cupido?
nempe deus, deus ille fuit, qui finibu' certis
sic alias aliis secernens, aequoris alti
inseruit freta salsa et dissociabile virus.

INDEX

(a) PROPER NAMES

INDEX

(b) SUBJECTS

INDEX

For EU product safety concerns, contact us at Calle de José Abascal, 56–1°, 28003 Madrid, Spain or eugpsr@cambridge.org.

 www.ingramcontent.com/pod-product-compliance
Ingram Content Group UK Ltd.
Pitfield, Milton Keynes, MK11 3LW, UK
UKHW012331130625
459647UK00009B/216